UNDERSTANDING
DESTRUCTIVE
RELATIONSHIPS

Personal and Family

By

Christine Corbett BA(Hons)
Dip.Hyp&Psych.

Printed and bound in Great Britain by:
The Cromwell Press Ltd
Wiltshire

Madion Press
Sussex

A CIP catalogue for this book is available from the British Library.

ISBN 0-9551111-1-0

Acknowledgements

Cover Art Design by Damion Corbett
Cover Head Design used by permission of Malcolm Thain
Line Drawings by Christine Corbett
Manuscript preparation by Gerald Law

I am grateful to Jon Bus, Editor of the Worthing Herald, for permission to précis reports from this newspaper

I am grateful to Caroline Brazier for permission to use concepts from her book "Buddhist Psychology"

Christine Corbett is the author of
    "UNDERSTANDING OURSELVES – WHY WE DO WHAT WE DO"
    (published by Madion Press ISBN 0-9551111-0-2)

This book is dedicated to the clients, friends, and acquaintances who told me their stories and gave me permission to use them in this book so that their experiences might help other people.

～   ～   ～

Contents

Introduction

The aim of this book is to help people who are in relationships they perceive as being destructive and to offer them an understanding of the psychology of the damaging person, and the damage inflicted on the victim.

Destructive relationships can create physical illness and mental distress.

When we are on the receiving end of destructive behaviour we will ask ourselves:

Why are they doing this to me?
What have I done to deserve this?

The short answer is usually "nothing". The destructive behaviour we are on the receiving end of is a game plan of the damaging person. The most damaging feature of the highly emotionally disturbed individual is that he or she will project their psychological disorder on to their victims – often telling them that they are mentally ill for being distressed at the abnormal behaviour which is been directed at them.

People have deeply ingrained personality characteristics and tend to behave the same way towards everyone they come into contact with. It is only other people's responses which are likely to change or moderate their behaviour.

I have used real-life stories and have attempted to explain the mechanics operating within damaging relationships, and I hope that people who are either in a destructive environment or have suffered through being in one, will find the information useful in coming to terms with their situation.

~ ~ ~

UNDERSTANDING DESTRUCTIVE
PERSONAL RELATIONSHIPS

THE BUILDING BLOCKS

OF

DESTRUCTIVE BEHAVIOUR

"How sweet I roamed from field to field

And tasted all the summer's pride

Till I the Prince of Love beheld

Who in the sunny beams did glide

He loves to sit and hear me sing

Then laughing sports and plays with me

He stretches out my golden wing

And mocks my loss of liberty".

William Blake

The eminent Psychiatrist, R D Laing believed:

> **"destructive behaviour is a direct result of a person**
> **having their experience destroyed".**

Freud claimed:

> **"so great is our impulse to destroy ourselves**
> **that we must destroy another person".**

It is worth considering that:

- ❖ **people who damage other people maliciously and deliberately are suffering from a serious personality defect**

- ❖ **people who damage other people are indiscriminate in who they hurt – victims should not take it personally**

- ❖ **destructive behaviour is based on "the compulsion to repeat" bad childhood experiences**

- ❖ **victims blame themselves**

~ ~ ~

Eric Berne, a prominent Psychiatrist and author of *"Games People Play"*, believed that people function on three different levels:

- ❖ **the child**

- ❖ **the adult**

- ❖ **the parent**

This can cause relationship problems when an immature partner treats the other as their parent and reacts against them as if they were their mother or father. He described "The Jerk" who is overly sensitive to parental influences. His ability to function as a thinking adult or his ability to be spontaneous like a child has been damaged at a critical point in childhood. This has resulted in inappropriate or clumsy behaviour in adulthood.

~   ~   ~

A Psychologist called Lawrence Kohlberg described three different levels of moral functioning:

Basic: this is purely satisfying the urge for self-gratification and avoiding de-
              tection and punishment.

              This could be described as being on the level of a small child.

Middle: this takes into account other people's feelings and welfare.

              People on this level are law-abiding.

              This could be described as being at the level of an adult.

Highest: this shows concern for other people's well-being but selects its own
              principles for living.

              This could be described as being on the level of a parent.

~   ~   ~

> **Sir Michael Rutter, the leading Psychiatrist,
> believes that a person's inherited personality
> traits cause the experiences they have. These
> traits then affect the way they react to the
> experiences they have created.**

Hans Eysenck, an eminent Psychologist, claimed that at least three quarters of a person's personality is inherited, and the rest is the result of environmental influences.

The child Psychologist, Jerome Kagan, claims that temperament "is a gift given to the newborn child by the genetic fairy godmother". He considers that a person's character – the way they conduct themselves in society – is formed by the environment.

American research has shown that certain "predispositions" have at least a 35% component of being inherited:

- ❖ sexual orientation

- ❖ alcoholism

- ❖ drug addiction

- ❖ "compulsive shopping"

- ❖ religiousness

- ❖ divorce

- ❖ political persuasion

- ❖ musical taste

- ❖ clothing

There is also some evidence to suggest that people act on subconscious instincts, which are then rationalized by another part of the brain half a second later. In other words, people act on impulse and then try to justify it. This would indicate that depending on the strength of a person's subconscious drives and their level of self-control, it is very difficult for many people to control their behaviour.

～   ～   ～

If a person suffers from a sudden and severe change in personality, apart from factors such as inherited illness or severe stress, it may be a result of:

❖ drink or drug abuse

❖ brain disease

❖ head injury

There was a reported case some years ago of a sportsman taking part in a fencing competition, when his opponent accidentally thrust his fencing foil up this man's nostril and it penetrated the frontal lobe of his brain. The man, on his recovery, experienced symptoms of severe depersonalisation, that is, feelings of unreality and of events in the world having a dream-like quality.

In another well-documented case, an American Railway worker in the 19th century sustained a head injury when he was using explosives as part of his work.

His personality changed from that of being very pleasant, jovial and cooperative, to being extremely aggressive and abusive. He changed from being a man of sober habits into being a drunk. This behaviour bordered on the psychopathic.

This led the medical profession to investigate whether head injury can substantially alter personality.

~　　　　~　　　　~

Many people suffer from what Psychologists call "Existential Anxiety" – or what could be described as a negative perspective on life. They believe life is essentially meaningless and they cannot believe that anything they do is valuable and useful. These people are also prone to depression and are emotionally bland.

Existential Psychologists believe that psychologically healthy people focus on the abstract and symbolic and live for today, while psychologically unhealthy individuals are highly materialistic and are always preparing for tomorrow.

A Psychologist called Carl Rogers believed that psychological disorders result from the fact that we are constantly judged by people close to us –our parents and our partners – the love and approval we receive from them is conditional.

To become aware of our own true feelings, we need relationships with people we see as approving of us unconditionally – loving us and approving of us without standing in judgment over us.

Mother Love is usually unconditional – mothers love their children while attempting to mould their behaviour into the good and acceptable.

Very many people go through their lives:

❖ trying to re-experience the unconditional love they got from their mothers with their partners

❖ expecting their partner to provide them with the unconditional love they believe they didn't get from their mother

❖ punishing their partners for the unconditional love they believe they were starved of in childhood

Even mother love is likely to be conditional as we grow older; we cannot expect to have our faults tolerated when we should be able to control our behaviour as adults.

It is naïve and immature to expect our parents and partners to provide us with unconditional love, particularly when our behaviour is damaging to them.

~   ~   ~

A great deal of destructive behaviour can be traced back to problems rooted in childhood. Personality traits (as are other inherited features) come through to the 3rd generation, that is, people inherit their grandparent's characteristics.

It is my belief that people are shaped
by the way their inherited personality
traits are handled by their parents
and other important adults such as
relatives and teachers.

This could be interpreted as:

* ❖ "bad men" could be tamed by strong women

* ❖ "good men" with weak personalities could be made bad by "bad women"

* ❖ "bad women" could be tamed by strong men

* ❖ "good women" with weak personalities could be made bad by "bad men".

~　　　~　　　~

* ❖ Good genes + good upbringing = succeeder

* ❖ Good genes + bad upbringing = survivor

* ❖ Bad genes + bad upbringing = loser/criminal/mental illness

* ❖ Bad genes + good upbringing = survivor.

Destructive people invariably have insight into their behaviour and this is displayed in their body language.

If someone really wants to change, there are psychological therapies which can assist.

Professional help can be very effective

SEXUAL LOVE

"True Love is but a humble, low-born thing.
And hath its food served up in earthen ware
It is a thing to walk with,
hand-in-hand
Through the everydayness of
this workday world."

James Russell Lowell

Relationship types

> *"How do I love thee? Let me count the ways*
> *I love thee to the depth and breadth and height*
> *My soul can reach, when feeling out of sight*
> *For the ends of being and ideal Grace"*
>
> *Charles Fenno Hoffman*

A Psychologist called Robert Sternberg believes there are three components to love – passion, intimacy and commitment.

He describes eight possible ways of combining these three ingredients:

Nonlove: this is the way we interact with other people on a day-to-day basis. People who are in marriages and sexual partnerships which function on this level need to have a good look at what is happening as the relationship is on very shaky ground.

Liking: there is little or no passion or commitment – but there is a high level of intimacy and couples on this level of functioning are operating like best friends.

Infatuation: the main ingredient of this is a high level of passion. Intimacy and commitment are low.

Empty Love: there is a high level of commitment. Passion and intimacy are virtually non-existent. This often involves 'staying together for the sake of the children'.

Romantic Love: this is a feature of new relationships. This is high on passion and intimacy but commitment has yet to be established.

Compassionate Love: this is high on intimacy and commitment but low on passion. This is often found in long married couples who are happy with each other but the sexual attraction has faded.

Fatuous Love: there is a high level of passion and commitment, but very little psychological intimacy. This type of relationship is based on sexual chemistry. The relationship may well founder when they discover they are incompatible or that they actually dislike each other.

Consummate Love: this is the ideal relationship with high levels of passion, intimacy and commitment.

~   ~   ~

Sex Differences

The Psychologists, Clyde and Susan Hendricks, researched the differences between men and women regarding their attitudes to sex. To narrow it down:

<u>**Men give love to get sex**</u>   <u>**Women give sex to get love**</u>

Men tend to have a much more permissive attitude towards sex; believing that:

❖ the best sex has no strings attached

❖ it is acceptable to manipulate someone into having sex as long as no promises to commitment are made.

These people are known as "Game Players" and they believe it is acceptable to deceive and manipulate sexual partners for the purpose of self gratification.

There is generally no intention of working towards an emotionally intimate relationship with the object of their sexual attraction.

Women tend to be more responsible. They believe that:

- ❖ It is necessary to have a meaningful relationship to have good sexual relations

- ❖ Sex should be the merging of two souls

"I gave her my heart but she wanted my soul"

Bob Dylan

The hypothalamus is the part of the brain which houses our primitive instincts. There is an area of the hypothalamus which, in men, is twice the size of a woman's.

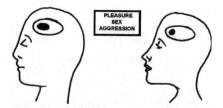

The different emotional needs of men and women

In his book *"Men are from Mars – Women are from Venus"*, John Gray claimed that:

Women need: caring, understanding, respect, devotion, validation, reassurance and to feel cherished

Men need: trust, acceptance, appreciation, admiration, approval, encouragement and to feel needed.

He believed these to be primary love needs.

It could be argued that emotional needs are not necessarily exclusively male and female. Surely, women need trust, appreciation and encouragement, and men must surely require understanding, devotion and reassurance.

Another important point to be considered, is that we must earn having our emotional needs met, and that the overwhelming love need is trust, because without trust there can be no solid basis for a relationship.

Making an equal contribution to the relationship in terms of responding to the other partner's emotional needs will create and maintain a sense of fairness. If one partner believes they are getting the "short end of the stick" – a raw deal – then they will feel very dissatisfied and seek to end the marriage.

An essential factor in establishing and maintaining a relationship is communication, and to avoid falling into "traditional" male/female stereotypes. No woman, and no man, likes to feel they are being lumped together with every woman or man on the planet and that they are in no way unique or special in their abilities or temperament.

There are different levels of men and women and they need to understand each other in the special context of their own personal relationship.

~   ~   ~

A Psychologist called Zick Rubin claimed that men are more likely to believe they should marry for love and disregard differences in attitudes and personality – the heart rules the head for men.

Men are more likely than women to want to fall in love. They are less likely to end a relationship and they suffer badly when a relationship ends.

The overall difference between men and women is that women are objective in seeing the wider picture, looking for situations in which to be in love such as weddings, children, family gatherings and family homes.

From my own observations I have noticed that the distinction between love and sex are very clear in men:

"Some women, well you want a good quality caring relationship with them. Other women are so beautiful you just want to ▆▆▆ their brains out", says Mike.

~   ~   ~

Freud believed that our choices of life partner are heavily influenced by our relationship with our parents.

Barbara has been married twice.

> *"The first time around, I think I married my father – a man with the same character traits of strength and authority, which I couldn't cope with. Although I found his taking control of everything made me feel secure, I also found it oppressive. I think that the second time around, I married my mother, with her weaknesses and lack of self-control, which I couldn't cope with either – this frightened me as all the responsibility lay on my shoulders."*

~   ~   ~

It has been my observation that many women find "deviant" men sexually attractive.

The real dream of a 35-year-old woman.

I dreamed I walked up the garden path of my house and the first thing I noticed was that the front door was broken open. I walked in-side and there was a room where men were talking and I wasn't al-lowed to go in: I felt frightened.

I went into another room where there was a piano which was cov-ered with a large heavy cloth. I wanted to take the cloth off the piano.

This dream represents a girl's emerging sexuality. Fear and sexuality are often combined and one emotion can feed off the other.

This woman related that when she was an 11-year-old girl her father was mixed up in gangland activities and there were often "meetings" in a special room in the house.

The sight of the gang members was both frightening and sexually arousing. The covered piano represents her dormant sexuality which would take the form of masturbation.

The broken front door is the wish-fulfilment of losing her virginity.

~   ~   ~

The most important factor in establishing and maintaining a good relationship is a sense of equity – that both parties make an equal contribution to the relation-ship. When one party does all the giving and the other does all the taking, then there will be extreme dissatisfaction.

When one party causes extreme upset to the other over a long period of time and then offers a small amount of compensation in return for causing profound emotional distress – the injured party becomes a victim and their status and self-esteem is destroyed.

It is likely that receiving compensation appropriate to the level of emotional injury sustained is likely to be a much better way of healing the relationship and restoring equity.

~   ~   ~

Jealousy

> **"The heart has its reasons which reason knows nothing of"**
>
> *Blaise Pascal*

The feelings of love can often be shadowed by anxiety, jealousy and sadness. This could be caused by psychological problems which have lain dormant since childhood.

Many lovers examine their worthiness for being accepted into that person's life.

There is a big difference between feeling insecure and feeling jealous. It is normal to feel insecure about a romantic relationship in its early stages.

Jealousy is angry and it is aggressive – it provokes action. Jealous people have low self-esteem, are nervous about life and see the world as a frightening place. This can become so intense that they border on paranoia.

Because jealous people have a negative concept of themselves they find it hard to believe a sexual partner could see some good in them. Jealousy destroys relationships, but some people believe it is possible to measure how much you love someone by how jealous you are.

Possessively jealous people treat their partners as though they are their own personal possession.

Fearfully jealous people cannot cope with being alone and feel rejected by this.

Competitively jealous people cannot cope with their partners being successful.

~   ~   ~

Love sickness

"Love is a pardonable insanity"

Sébastien Chamfort

Psychologists believe that there are similarities between love and mental illness.

Robert Sternberg described lovesickness as "an infatuation which is characterized by obsession, irrational idealisation, emotional instability and emotional dependency".

It can take the form of:

❖ **mania:**

extreme happiness, inflated self-esteem, extravagant present giving

❖ **depression:**

crying a lot, sleeplessness, lack of concentration.

❖ **obsessive- compulsive disorder:**

being preoccupied, checking all things, "over-the-top" hygiene rituals, hoarding of "knick-knacks".

When people "fall in love" their brain chemistry can change and this can produce the symptoms of depression.

The 10th century Iranian physician, "Avicenna", said the main symptom and cause of lovesickness is obsession.

～   ～   ～

WOMAN HATING

"Sigh no more ladies, sigh no more

Men were deceivers ever

One foot in the sea and one on the shore

To one thing constant never

Then sigh not so

But let things go

And be you blithe and bonny

Converting all your sounds of woe

Into Hey Nonny Nonny"

Much Ado about Nothing

William Shakespeare

Pornography

Wilhelm Reich was a pupil of Freud. He believed that a dissatisfied sexuality keeps our thoughts revolving around sex all the time. A satisfying and fulfilling sex life leaves our minds free for other things.

Men are frightened of their own sexuality. They fear their masculine identity will wither away and dissolve if they acknowledge that women also have strong sexual urges. Because they are still carrying with them fear of castration from early childhood, they become bullies and tyrants in their personal relationships. There are still carrying around with them deep-seated feelings of anxiety and panic.

A method of coping with this is to separate the emotions of affection and sexual attraction. They deny their sexual partner full sexual expression so that the caring and nurturing aspects of love become less full of dread. This is the basis of sexism. Both fear and sexuality release adrenaline.

Women's hairiness is connected with a female sexual power. Young men are often shocked to discover that females have body hair, particularly pubic hair. This resembles the way they imagined their own genitals would look, if they had been castrated as children.

The demands by women for full social, sexual and political equality are some of the most terrifying demands that men have had to deal with and create in them a sense of panic anxiety.

~   ~   ~

Germaine Greer, in her groundbreaking book *"The Female Eunuch"*, described the concept of "■■ hatred", whereby men have a deep-rooted distaste and disgust of the female sex organs. She claimed that "█████" is the worst swear word that someone can use towards another person.

Other words to describe the female sex organs are also very unflattering. This reduces the part of the body by which women give pleasure, conceive and give birth to future generations, to the level of a piece of meat.

A man's penis is described in terms of tools and weapons. These are related to objects which can control and destroy. K.A. Scherner, a Philosopher, claimed that to dream of weapons and tools represented masculinity: (this was before Freud).

The sex act is often described as █████, screwing, rooting, shagging – these words have connotations with power and violence – acts performed on a passive female.

Freud also described the sexual symbolism of dreaming of knives which relates to penetration.

~   ~   ~

According to Desmond Morris, sexually inferior men need either to degrade women or to see them degraded sexually. Very sexually inferior men require very degrading material or actual sexual activities.

Freud believed that the compulsion to look at pornography is a symptom of the immature male.

"Soft pornography" shows the breasts. This relates to "breast envy". The larger the breasts a man feels he needs to see, the more envy is expressed. This stems back to sibling rivalry in the early years of childhood. The mother's breasts look very large to a two year old in the "oral stage". The child has now been weaned from the breast and feels intensely jealous of the new infant who is a rival for his mother's affection. He feels pushed out and rejected, craving to return to his mother's breast.

The models and actresses usually adopt poses which appear to invite the viewer to have access to their over-inflated breasts without fear of rejection or competition from younger brothers and sisters.

"Medium pornography" shows women with their breasts and genitals exposed. It offers the viewer access to the breasts and also is an invitation to sexual intercourse. This can be interpreted as an opportunity to return to the womb with the comfort of the nipple in the mouth.

The models and actresses usually adopt poses which are familiar in the animal kingdom, particularly with chimpanzees where the rump is raised and the front of the body is lowered. This is a sign of submission to the male.

"Couples pornography", showing sexual intercourse is considered to be vicarious (performed for another) enjoyment of "taboo" sexual activity. The man – the father figure – is enjoying sexual activity with a woman – the mother figure. This stems from an intense desire at puberty to watch parents having sexual intercourse. This is coupled with a sense of intense distaste and disbelief that parents can engage in sexual activity. It is also a "latent" (lying dormant) desire to penetrate the mother which is too threatening to bring to consciousness because of the fear of castration and the deep-rooted fear that the vagina may have teeth as a punishment for that desire.

The viewer has the satisfaction of watching the actor have sexual intercourse with his penis remaining intact.

"Hardcore pornography" includes violent pornography showing sadomaso-chism, enslavement and generally violent sex.

The viewer has a deep-rooted inferiority complex and needs to achieve power by vicarious sexual tyranny.

"Cunnilingus" is a taboo area unlikely to be performed by the viewer as the female genitals represent a threat – possibly the loss of the tongue. This may be related to threats of having the tongue cut off or the mouth washed out for swearing as a child.

"Fellatio" is a fear of the female genitals creating a desire for the release of sperm into the mouth. This relates to a subconscious fear that the vagina may contain hidden teeth – which is a projection of "castration anxiety".

The mouth has visible teeth and the viewer can see the actor's penis going into the mouth and coming out in one piece.

"Spit roasting" (Mènage á trois) is a slang word for two men and one woman engaging in sexual activity.

The desire to watch this type of sexual activity relates to an "unresolved Oedi-pus Complex" where a man still has hang-ups from his childhood about being castrated for desiring his mother. He is still, subconsciously, a small boy in com-petition with his father.

Andrea Dworkin criticized pornography:

- ❖ it harms and exploits the women who take part in it

- ❖ it reinforces the myth that women like to be dominated by men

- ❖ it depicts degrading and humiliating images of women

- ❖ there is a probable link with sexual violence

- ❖ it can encourage direct imitation of pornographic scenes.

Research has shown there is a strong link between exposure to violent pornography and a tendency towards rape and sexual aggression.

～　　　　～　　　　～

It is not always necessarily the case that this degradation of women is always related to sex. Often men feel intellectually and emotionally inferior to women and they feel threatened by an educated woman who has strong emotional bonds with family and friends. The tactics they use may take the form of:

- ❖ belittling their partner's intelligence in social situations

- ❖ doing things to sabotage anything intelligent they may do

- ❖ competing with them, that is sex appeal versus intelligence, by dropping hints about extramarital activities they have had or are having when their partner engages in intelligent conversation.

- ❖ isolating their partners emotionally, psychologically and often geographically from their loved ones.

In this way they hope to break down strong intelligent female partners who challenge their male ego and make them, they believe, appear inferior to their female partners.

Women's perspectives

It is a common false belief that feminists hate men.

Women tend to hate men who hate women

To be at the receiving end of "sexist" abuse from men who are intellectually and socially inferior to the women they are abusing can only be described as intolerable. This is designed to degrade and humiliate.

Men's sexuality tends to be focused on the visual – "*I like the look of that – I'll make a move on it*", says Nick. Most women require some form of emotional commitment. For woman a good sex life is based on psychological intimacy. Feminists believe that a good sex education is necessary for someone to establish and maintain a good relationship. Very many "men's magazines" focus purely on the self-gratification aspects of sex and there is little or no emphasis on information or education into how to pleasure and satisfy a woman.

Many women's magazines emphasize the necessity of pleasing a man, although this has moved forward from the way they were many years ago. Even when the general theme is on women's sexual pleasure, the emphasis is on "teaching your man to please you". A woman's desire for a good sex life is not new. In 1839 a marriage manual blamed a female's "excessive ardour of desire" on male sterility.

Feminism is about more than sexual values. It is about promoting "traditionally female values" such as constructive attitudes, like sharing and cooperation; as opposed to "traditionally male values" such as competition and destructiveness.

Freud commented "War is menstruation envy".

The Male Ego

Men tend to invalidate women's feelings and find difficulty in either accepting or admitting they are wrong. They usually have to be pressurized into admitting wrongdoing.

Chris Rock, the "stand-up comedian" related an account in his show of how he had been caught cheating on his partner and stated his surprise that after accumulating all the evidence she required a confession, let alone an apology. He also stated that because he cheated on her, he didn't trust her.

Many men, when having badly damaged their partners, refer to it as "what happened" as though they had no control over their actions. What they should accept is the context of "what they did" which is often done in a premeditated way.

Men often have a deep-rooted sense of inferiority, feeling the need to prove themselves to other men and to impress them with their sexual conquests. Their sense of sexual inferiority may well reach its peak when their sons become sexually active.

Sexism can also relate to fathers and daughters, with fathers encouraging their sons is to be high achieving, whilst actively discouraging their daughters from being successful in what they feel should be a male dominated world.

It appears that many men find it difficult to cope with the idea that women can be "better than them" and will do everything in their power to crush and destroy their female "loved one's" achievements and successes in order to protect their own very weak sense of self-esteem, which tends to be dependent on status, money and power.

Men expect to be forgiven for their mistakes, yet find it difficult to forgive their partners. They seem unable to take their own behaviour into account when their partner makes a mistake.

Sometimes men marry a dominant woman who is a "surrogate father figure" and who makes them feel secure. At the same time he lives in fear of her wrath and seeks to defy her and do bad things behind her back.

Despite some decades of "female emancipation", many men's attitudes towards women appear to have remained stagnant and entrenched.

≈   ≈   ≈

IDENTIFYING DAMAGED PEOPLE

"...I am only by Love designed

to be the victim for mankind"

John Dryden

Handwriting analysis

Hans Eysenck carried out research into handwriting analysis and claimed that Graphologists were 67% accurate in their assessments of people's personalities.

I have also carried out my own study into the accuracy of handwriting analysis using a sample of 100 clerical workers. The feedback from the people themselves revealed a 98% level of accuracy.

How to identify damaged people using handwriting analysis.

ꞷ	= w – in need of emotional protection
ı	= I (capital letter – very small) low esteem
ἰ	= i (dash instead of dot over i) anxiety, anger and resentment
ɟ	= g - weakness, timidity
A	= A - disappointment
t	= t - weak health
ʍʍʑ	= m – torn character

Anxiety

Many people in damaging relationships find themselves suffering from a condition called **"Generalized Anxiety Disorder"**. They will feel:

❖ plagued by unrealistic worries which are blown out of all proportion virtually on a daily basis

❖ restlessness: being keyed up and on edge

❖ easily fatigued

❖ difficulty in concentrating

❖ irritable, with muscle tension

❖ unable to get a good night's sleep

❖ as if there is a tight elastic band around the head.

In its acute form it can take the form of a full-blown panic attack where a person experiences:

❖ a pounding heart with rapid heartbeat

❖ sweating

❖ trembling or shaking

❖ shortness of breath and/or a feeling of being suffocated

❖ feeling of choking

❖ chest pain or discomfort

❖ feeling sick with pain in the gut

❖ feeling light-headed, dizzy or faint

❖ feelings of unreality or being detached from themselves

❖ feeling they are losing control or going mad

❖ a true belief that they are going to die

❖ numbness or tingling sensations

❖ icy chills or hot flushes.

Often a panic attack is so severe and distressing that it can be mistaken for a heart attack. The frequent experience of having panic attacks in public places often leads to agoraphobia, and a panic attack in a public place will intensify if that person hasn't got a companion for support.

The symptoms of anxiety or a full-blown panic attack may also be the symptoms of a physical illness and it is important that people experiencing these unpleasant symptoms consult with a GP before diagnosing themselves as suffering from anxiety.

~   ~   ~

Depression

Symptoms of depression

Depressed people persistently have a tendency to feel:

❖ sad, empty and tearful

❖ a lack of interest or pleasure in activities

❖ the need to over-eat or under-eat

❖ suffering from insomnia or oversleep

❖ either restless or immobile

❖ they have little energy and feel tired all the time

❖ they have feelings of worthlessness

❖ they have feelings of excessive and inappropriate guilt

❖ a lack of concentration and are indecisive

❖ recurring thoughts of death, with strong suicidal impulses, even to the extent of planning suicide.

Some types of depression stem from a sense of learned helplessness. This can be a direct result of being in a destructive relationship. It can mean feeling trapped and being in prison. Each way you turn you meet a brick wall. Retreat into despair can often be the only coping mechanism.

The damaging person may thrive on the fact that their partner is in such a vulnerable state. It could well enhance their sense of power.

The depressed person may over-eat, drink heavily or take drugs. People in a state of "learned helplessness" can often become suicidal.

Unlike the other types of depression, which are often inherited or caused by traumatic childhood events, "learned helplessness" can be relieved by taking direct steps to change the existing situation, with the assistance of professional help.

The most overwhelming feature of "learned helplessness" is a loss of power. It is essential that the sufferer learns, or rekindles, a lost sense of empowerment. The most effective form of empowerment is assertiveness–

dealing with the root cause of the problem

~   ~   ~

Depersonalisation

This may be caused by acute stress or emotional anxiety caused by being in a damaging relationship. "Depersonalized" people may:

❖ find themselves somewhere without knowing how they got there

❖ find things in their possession they don't remember buying

❖ feel they are:

      standing next to themselves

      watching themselves

      seeing themselves as if they were looking at another person

❖ fail to recognize family and friends

❖ feel that people and the world around them are not real

❖ feel their body does not belong to them

❖ find their reactions to things vary so wildly that they could be two different people

❖ hear voices in their heads:

      telling them to do things

      commenting on the things they are doing.

Some sufferers can self-mutilate in an attempt to 'feel' themselves.

        ~   ~   ~

Paranoid Feelings

"Conspiracy theory" has it that "just because you're paranoid, it does not mean the bastards aren't out to get you".

Francis Bacon (before Shakespeare) claimed "Suspicions amongst thoughts are like bats amongst birds – they ever fly by twilight"…"They dispose kings to tyranny, husbands to jealousy, wise men to… melancholy".

The main features of paranoia are:

❖ a person believes in general that they will come to harm

❖ they have identified a persecutor who is going to harm them

In identifying true paranoia it is important to determine whether the feelings of persecution are real or unfounded.

~   ~   ~

IDENTIFYING DAMAGING PEOPLE

"Know thyself, presume not God to scan
The proper study of mankind is Man

...

With too much knowledge for the sceptic side
With too much weakness for the stoic's pride
He hangs between, in doubt to act or rest
In doubt to deem himself a god or beast."

Alexander Pope

Handwriting analysis

How to identify damaging people using handwriting analysis.

t = t - psychological brutality

= g - aggression due to sexual frustration

= g - physical violence and mental cruelty

= g - very aggressive traits: hostile nature: cold hearted and narrow-minded

= o - secretiveness

I love you   = (the printed word) – difficulty in feeling love

= selfish, lustful and lowered resistance to sexual excesses and perversions: violent

= t - emotional hypersensitivity

= t - tendency to ill treat others

= C - pre-occupation with sexual instincts; inflated sexual imagination, exaggerated sexual urges; tendency towards sexual perversions

= f - resentful, with odd sexual behaviour

= g - abnormal sexual interests

Strategies damaging people use to protect themselves and manipulate people.

- ❖ Deviousness

- ❖ Secretiveness

- ❖ Being manipulative

- ❖ Abnormally high demands for love and affection

- ❖ Nit-picking – demanding exact dates and times for misdemeanours they are accused of

- ❖ Running away from confrontation

- ❖ Deceit

- ❖ Sarcasm disguised as compliments

- ❖ Treachery disguised as kindness

- ❖ The "dripping tap" of emotional abuse

- ❖ Making fun of other people

- ❖ Causing emotional pain

- ❖ Poisoning other people's minds against their victims.

"Ruses" - games for getting off the hook for wrongdoing.

- ❖ Pretending they don't know what you are talking about when confronted

❖ Feigning affront and indignation when confronted with wrongdoing

❖ Claiming that you are mad for accusing them of doing wrong

❖ Claiming other people think you are mad for accusing them of doing wrong

❖ Admitting to wrongdoing at the time when you are unable to do any-thing about it and denying it later

❖ Giving you a multitude of reasons for what is wrong with them except for the real reason, that is, that they are a very flawed character.

Research has shown that personality disorders are caused by a combination of inherited personality traits and personal experience. It has been found that per-sonality problems tend to be clumped together in certain families.

In some families the abnormal behaviour will take the form of alcoholism, in oth-ers it will be antisocial behaviour. Antisocial behaviour is much more common in men and Borderline Personality Disorder is much more common in women.

Researchers have discovered that people with Personality Disorders may be suffering from Post-Traumatic Stress Disorder caused by terrifying childhood experiences.

Between the ages of 3 and 7 is the period in which the brain is thought to be shaped by learning good social skills such as:

❖ the ability to have self control

❖ the ability to calm down when upset

❖ the ability to concentrate

At around the age of 5 years children are believed to have the ability to plan their activities.

Personality Disorder is considered to be a treatable condition.

Pathological lying

The pathological liar will lie to everyone about everything.

"Normal" people will lie to protect themselves and other people's feelings and sometimes for self-benefit, providing no harm is caused.

Pathological lying is a power mechanism – the power being in the ability to deceive.

The power mechanisms involved can be:

❖ the need to cause emotional pain

❖ the need to humiliate

❖ the need to degrade

These are probably extensions of childhood trauma and an overwhelming sense of inferiority. These negative emotions could have been caused by:

❖ position in the family

❖ poverty

❖ physical impairment

These factors could create an uncontrollable desire for the victim to experience the same level of suffering they were subjected to as children.

Pathological lying can be a symptom of psychopathic behaviour.

~   ~   ~

How to identify a liar

When a person is replying to an intrusive question:

❖ their eyes will go up to the **left** when they are telling the truth

❖ their eyes will go up to the **right** when they are lying

Other aspects of body language are revealing about someone who is lying:

❖ touching the face is a sign of a person having negative feelings about themselves

❖ wooden body posture

❖ flat monotone voice

❖ lack of eye contact

❖ looking down to the floor or the ground or covering their eyes with their hands indicates shame

❖ scratching or picking their faces shows self-blame.

~   ~   ~

The Inferiority Complex

Alfred Adler, an eminent Psychologist, believed that people have a concept called "Will to Power" which they use to compensate themselves for feelings of Inferiority.

It is likely that the Power Games that people play stem from a strong sense of inferiority, usually originating in childhood experience.

Alice Miller, a prominent Psychoanalyst, gives this example of how a sense of inferiority is formed in childhood.

When she was on holiday she saw couple with their child. The adults were each eating a large ice cream cone and the child wanted one. His mother offered him a bite of hers, but he wanted the whole ice cream so she withdrew it from him completely.

The child was crying and his parents were laughing at him.

A person with an inferiority complex:

- ❖ cannot cope with constructive criticism and calls it "character assassination"

- ❖ blames other people for what is wrong with him or her

- ❖ feels persecuted for no good reason to the extent she or he becomes paranoid

- ❖ looks for faults in other people to make him or herself look good in comparison

- ❖ avoids competition

- ❖ avoids social contact with other people.

Another symptom of low self-esteem is belittling: this involves trashing the other person in public in order to achieve increased personal status for themselves.

People with low self-esteem and an inferiority complex are likely to be depressed, irritable and/or aggressive. They have feelings of resentment, alienation and unhappiness. They are likely to suffer from insomnia and psychosomatic symptoms. Arrogance may be a way of disguising low self-esteem.

Passive aggression

The "passive-aggressive" person has a lot of the traits of the emotional vampire, which takes the form of viciousness; saying and doing unpleasant things when the victim cannot fight back. These people lack confidence and cannot cope either with being confronted with anything or confronting people. This is also a form of cowardice.

These people act in an underhand way. This can take the form of deliberately "forgetting" to do something important for someone who has upset them – rather than confronting them outright. Sabotage is also the weapon of the passive-aggressive person.

The anal personality

This is a particularly destructive person.

The anal personality is mean, ruthless and shallow. These people are obsessed by order, routine and discipline. They are vain and materialistic. They seek to have power over other people and brood when upset. They are jealous and suspicious. Emotional Vampirism is their main weapon – they are physical and mental sadists, having a strong need to inflict suffering on other people. This is often the result of suffering they believe they experienced as children. These people are not necessarily psychopaths – often feeling remorse for their behaviour and attempting to offer compensation to those they hurt. They are "normal" people with a very nasty side to their nature.

Sensation seeking

Marvin Zuckerman of the University of Delaware has spent many years re-searching a personality trait called "Sensation Seeking".

Sensation seeking people are always looking for activities which involve some degree of physical risk, such as mountaineering, abseiling or parachuting. These people have few restraints on their behaviour and would not be averse to wife-swapping, drug-taking or heavy drinking at wild parties. Sensation seekers do not feel bound by conventional standards of morality, are bored by routine and are always looking for a buzz.

In its positive form sensation seeking can produce positive reactions to chal-lenges and sensation seekers can be adventurers or discoverers and generally "go to places where no man has been before".

In its negative form these people can become criminals and drug addicts and lead a decadent lifestyle.
Sensation seeking is believed to be hereditary.

~   ~   ~

Intermittent Explosive Disorder

People with this disorder are chronically impulsive and very violent. When feel-ing threatened they display violence which is excessive and totally out of relation to the level of provocation involved.

This disorder is believed either to be caused by a head injury or is inherited.

~   ~   ~

Paranoid Personality Disorder

This condition differs from paranoid schizophrenia as the sufferer is in touch with reality but has a distorted perspective on other people and their relationships with them.

- ❖ they suspect, without sufficient basis in fact, that other people are deceiving them, exploiting them or are out to harm them

- ❖ they doubt the trustworthiness or loyalty of the people close to them

- ❖ they cannot confide in others because of an unwarranted fear that the information will be used against them

- ❖ they read hidden negative or threatening messages into innocent remarks or events

- ❖ they persistently bear grudges and are unforgiving of people who cause them even the slightest harm

- ❖ they believe people are continually attacking their character and re-act angrily

- ❖ they are suspicious without justification of the fidelity of their sexual partner.

～   ～   ～

Borderline Personality Disorder

People with this disorder appear arrogant with an overdeveloped sense of power and importance – they fancy themselves and often people of the same sex – Narcissism. This can be a defence against intense psychological instability (neuroticism), which is inherited, and also low self-esteem.

People with this disorder have intense, stormy and short-lived relationships where their partners are alternately put on a pedestal and then crushed under foot. They are prone to having affairs, blaming their partners for their unfaithfulness, believing that what they don't know won't hurt them. Their affairs are part of a game-playing ritual even to the extent that they actually believe their own lies. This is the main feature of this disorder.

On the other side of the coin they can often suffer from depression and mood swings, and fear being left alone, seeing this as being abandoned. They are often self-harming and seriously suicidal having negative feelings about themselves. They are dependant and self-critical.

They are argumentative, irritable and sarcastic. Their behaviour is unpredictable and impulsive, often with eating, gambling, spending and sex sprees. They can also have psychopathic traits.

Sufferers cannot cope with reality and have paranoid convictions that others are hostile and malicious. They generally view other people as destructive and fickle. They have a very weak ego.

This disorder is believed to be the borderline between neurotic illness and schizophrenia.

Borderline Personality Disorder starts in adolescence, tends to run in families and the neurotic part of the illness is an inherited condition. It is most often found in families where there are high levels of conflict and low levels of affection. These families are likely to be physically and sexually abusing, creating emotionally traumatized children.

People suffering from this condition are not considered suitable for conventional psychoanalysis but benefit from a certain type of therapy where the patient's behaviour is accepted by the therapist with "unconditional regard" and then modified by focusing on solving problems and promoting better interpersonal skills.

The Sociopath

Sociopaths are not considered to be psychologically disturbed but their behaviour is generally deviant.

A young person fitting this category is grossly selfish, callous, impulsive and irresponsible. The sociopath tends to be involved in "rather illegal activities", has "skirmishes" with the police and is continually in trouble with others.

The signs of sociopathy usually start with truancy from school and minor scrapes with the law. These people often get involved with conning other people out of money and goods and have very low levels of guilt and anxiety, which in "normal people" prevent anti-social and deviant behaviour. These people tend to have a pronounced sense of fearlessness and are generally considered to be under- socialized.

The sociopath differs from the delinquent, in that unlike the delinquent he has no group to belong to, but is a loner taking what he can, unable to feel any sense of loyalty to a person or group of people.

Sociopaths tend to come from families where this tendency is well-established, where there is an alcoholic father and where standards of discipline are inconsistent or completely lacking.

~   ~   ~

Derek is a sociopath. He truly believes it is acceptable to lie, cheat and steal providing he doesn't get caught. Derek has had to go to court on several occasions for theft, but he still persists in stealing, mainly petty theft in the form of shoplifting. Derek does it for the buzz – not actually wanting what he steals, but enjoying the adrenaline high of the act of theft. It gives him smug satisfaction to know he is getting something for nothing.

Derek thinks his wayward ways are "funny". It's all a big joke to him – a game he plays with other people's lives and he is genuinely surprised that they don't see the funny side of it. He regards himself as a "lovable rogue" rather than a very heavily flawed character.

Some of Derek's pals have been known to remark "Derek thinks "decency" is a brand of wine and "fidelity" a brand of sound system".

Derek suffers from anxiety, and sometimes this explodes into "hysterical behaviour": he drinks heavily to overcome feelings of low self-worth in social situations.

Derek attempts to compensate his wife, not for the hurt he has caused her, but to stop her divorcing him so he doesn't lose everything he has worked for. The compensation usually takes the form of sex and money – his own yardsticks – and he is genuinely surprised that she is not impressed by what is on offer.

Derek's upbringing was what could be described as average – being the second child of four he had to take responsibility for his younger brothers as a child. There was always fierce competition for his mother's time and affection. Derek's father spent a lot of time at work and his main rôle was of breadwinner and disciplinarian. However, this family situation was normal for boys growing up in Derek's generation and very many of his friends and acquaintances turned out well.

What Derek's wife actually needs and wants is honesty, trust and kindness. Mainly she needs compassion in times of need, not the combination of immaturity and self-pity he displays when he sees her not being able to cope with overwhelming problems. He hasn't got the mentality to show empathy – to understand where she is "coming from".

Everything that Derek is he hangs on others. This is known as "Attribution Theory". He attributes all his wants, needs and shortcomings on to other people: he truly believes other people have the same wants, needs and shortcomings that he does.

Derek expects love and affection in return for lies, deceit and adultery.

Because Derek has such low self-esteem he is constantly seeking reassurance from his wife that he is loved and that he is worthy of love.

If his wife is preoccupied with other matters and can't find enough time for him, he takes this as meaning she doesn't love him any more. He has to have his ego massaged and his self-esteem reinforced on a continual basis, otherwise he starts to experience the overwhelming feelings of emotional emptiness that he felt as a child when competing for his mother's affections with his brothers and sister, and the sense of low self-worth associated with this.

Derek's wife is very intelligent. Because he can't make her feel inferior intellectually he makes her feel inferior sexually by always comparing her appearance unfavourably with that of other women. He wants to make her feel as inferior as he does.

Although Derek does low-paid manual work he has a "James Bond complex" whereby he tries to impress women by dressing himself up in expensive suits and drinking vodka martinis.

This is done to overcome his deep-seated feelings of inferiority. Money is Derek's God and it allows him to buy himself status. Without the "window dressing" Derek is so shallow he could be transparent.

As a child he was always in trouble at school. One minute he would be fooling around and then someone would upset him, possibly another pupil or the teacher telling him to pay attention to his school-work (which was always below average) and then he would fly into a furious rage.

In childhood Derek did not have much in the way of toys and clothes as his parents were poor. Birthdays and Christmas were really a non-event in that money was very tight and although his parents did their best they could not afford to buy much for Derek compared to what other children were getting. This created a great sense of inferiority in Derek – particularly in financial terms and his main motives throughout all of his adult life are to acquire money and material possessions.

Throughout their married life Derek has been particularly mean with his wife when it comes to birthdays and Christmas – obtaining some type of perverse satisfaction from telling his wife that he cannot afford to buy her much for a present as they have heavy financial commitments. However there is always sufficient money for Derek to buy himself what he wants.

Everything Derek's wife does that is good and decent, he sabotages. She has said to him, "Everything that is good and decent you have destroyed". He has replied with a combined air of self-loathing and self-pity. *"I've destroyed your life – I must be on self-destruct!"*

So great is his impulse to destroy himself – he must destroy someone else.

Derek is profoundly jealous of anyone who appears to have a warm, happy relationship with their partners and families and he sets out to destroy these relationships.

He is jealous of his own children because his wife obviously loves them. He is jealous of his wife because her mother loves her and displays it constantly.

~   ~   ~

The sociopath differs from the psychopath in the respect that sociopaths, whilst living on the fringes of the law, confine their activities to petty theft

and minor scrapes; whereas the psychopath tends to be remorselessly involved in serious offences involving cruelty to other people and is suffering from a very serious personality defect.

~   ~   ~

The Psychopath
**Underneath a superficial veneer of charm and friendliness lies a very
dangerous animal.**

**A Psychopath is a moral defective, a person who has no moral principles
and does not fear punishment.**

~   ~   ~

The Mental Health Act of 1959 described the Psychopath as someone who indulges in abnormally aggressive or seriously irresponsible conduct and later
Mental Health Acts consider it to be a mental illness.

Two schools of thought operate as to what circumstances create a psychopath:

- ❖ Faulty brain wiring connecting the "planning" area and the "conscience", creating lack of restraint and failure to feel remorse

- ❖ Lack of maternal affection in the first year of childhood.

~   ~   ~

A German Psychiatrist named Koch believed that Psychopaths have an inbuilt
predisposition to be neurotic. He decided that they displayed:

- ❖ **abnormalities and eccentricities of behaviour**

- ❖ **behaviour caused by anxiety states.**

He called this "Psychopathic Inferiority".

He also described "the hereditary transmission of the 'taint of insanity'" and this referred particularly to:

❖ alcoholism

❖ sexual promiscuity.

~   ~   ~

Francis Gall, who founded Phrenology, claimed that "moral insanity" was caused by a derangement of the part of the brain concerned with making the choice between good and evil.

There are two major clusters of psychopathic behaviour.

❖ **Emotional Detachment**

Selfishness

Lack of remorse and exploiting other people

Callousness

Lack of empathy

Conning people

Manipulating people

❖ **Antisocial Lifestyle**

Parasitic behaviour – living off other people

Pathological lying

History of Juvenile Delinquency

~   ~   ~

The Psychologists, Curran and Mallison, described three major classes of Psychopathic personality:

❖ **the "vulnerable" – see themselves as a victim**

❖ **the "unusual" – the odd bod – does strange things**

❖ **the "sociopathic" – the petty thief**

The vulnerable psychopath has a low capacity for coping with the ordinary stresses and strains of everyday life and is likely to suffer from neurotic illnesses such as anxiety and phobic states.

～　　　～　　　～

"Psychopath" is a term often applied to young males who appear unable to conform to the rules of society.

These young men:

❖ Are unable to tolerate minor frustrations

❖ Are unable to form stable relationships

❖ Fail to learn from past experiences however unpleasant they are

❖ Tend to act impulsively or recklessly.

The psychopath completely lacks the ability to relate to another person's feelings.

Research carried out in England – "The Hare Psychopathy Checklist" – shows that we cannot instil an ability to relate to other people's feelings or a strengthened conscience in psychopaths, but there is some possibility of altering their impulsivity, stimulation seeking and irresponsibility

Koch believed that these people can respond to firm but sympathetic handling in a disciplined environment. The "permissive" approach does not work: they lack the inner controls normally developed in childhood and adolescence.

～　　　～　　　～

A Psychologist called Harvey Checkley focuses the symptoms of the psychopath more on personality than behaviour.

He believes:

Psychopaths have a poverty of emotions both positive
and negative

He claims that psychopaths have no sense of shame – their so-called "positive
feelings" are merely an act and that they lack the negative emotions that make it
possible to learn from their mistakes. Their anti-social behaviour is performed
merely for the buzz.

~   ~   ~

Marvin is a psychopath – he gets off on seeing other people – particularly women, suffer emotional pain.

The overriding features of Marvin's personality are self-gratification
and self-protection, combined with a complete lack of remorse for
any harm he may cause. The only person Marvin sees as being a
victim is himself and his only emotion is self-pity. All of his behaviour
is premeditated and carefully calculated to gain the highest degree of
self-gratification and damage to other people. He is completely devoid of compassion.

Fear of punishment is not a deterrent for Marvin as he so arrogant he
doesn't believe he will be caught and punished for the things he
does. He has been caught red-handed in criminal acts but he ration-
alizes what he does to other people believing he has done nothing
wrong. He believes it is the people accusing him of wrong-doing who
are at fault and he tries to persuade other people that this is the

case. Everybody in the world has something wrong with them, except him. When he has been apprehended and punished for his crimes, he re-offends almost instantly – the punishments have no effect – there is zero learning curve. He has no control over his behaviour.

Marvin is a pathological and compulsive liar – he gets off on deceit, which is his main power mechanism. He also poisons people's minds against each other if he feels they are getting in the way of him satisfying his impulses for self-gratification.

His main driving forces in life are sex and money and he will stop at nothing to get these. Another strategy he uses is projecting an air of friendliness, and humbling himself to others in order to break down any emotional barriers they may have erected against him. Once he has done this, he uses "Emotional Vampirism" to its full extent. The weaker and more vulnerable the person, the harder he kicks them.

Despite the fact that Marvin suffers from panic attacks and claustrophobia and has a stress-related bowel disorder, he persists in his life of reckless impulsiveness.

Marvin gets a sense of smug satisfaction from cheating on his wife – he behaves as though this is an act of defiance. Because his wife was, at one stage in her life preoccupied with serious family problems, he initiated a sexual relationship with another woman. He blamed his wife for this, saying that she drove him to it. He gets immense pleasure out of telling his wife how much he loves the other woman and giving her a 'blow by blow' account of their sexual acts. He then gets an equal buzz out of telling the other woman how much he loves his wife. To use Marvin's own words, *"I'm killing two birds with one stone"*.

When the "other woman" is assaulted by her husband Marvin blames his wife, insisting that she helps his lover by contacting the Domestic Violence Helpline. When his wife throws him out of the house for the harm his extramarital relationship is causing to her health, he blames the other woman.

Marvin is emotionally hypersensitive – he reacts very strongly to anything he perceives to be emotional rejection. He is like this mainly with his wife, but also with everybody else he comes into contact with. This is mainly genetic, as both of his brothers are like this, but there is also an input from childhood experience when his mother used withdrawal of love as a method of discipline.

Despite all attempts by his wife to get him to understand her feelings, Marvin finds it impossible to relate to what he has put her through. His behaviour is reinforced by his mother who thinks her son is truly wonderful and can see no wrong in him.

Marvin tries to socially isolate his wife by trying to get her to make disparaging comments about other people within their earshot. What he will do is to whisper a comment of a derogatory nature about another person, and then trick her into confirming it when they are passing by.

Not content in trying to break down his wife single-handedly, he also poisons other people's minds against her. He feels justified in his behaviour towards his wife, particularly, as his perception of his own behaviour is distorted, even to the extent of believing his own lies.

Another of Marvin's strategies is to buy presents for the other woman and leave the bag and receipt lying around for his wife to find and then to insult her intelligence by offering an implausible lie as an explanation. His intention is to degrade and humiliate her. So strong are his psychopathic traits, that he will persist in what he is doing until his wife breaks down. Marvin gloats at the emotional power he has exercised and this gives him a very strong sense of satisfaction.

What Marvin is actually doing to other people is what he fears most himself. It is almost like a pre-emptive strike, to do it to them before they do to him. He is truly and utterly self-centred and has absolutely no morals or conscience, but has constructed his own personal set of rules for the way he lives, which are "go for what you want and don't get caught".

As a child Marvin experienced immense pleasure in pulling the legs of insects and inflicting cruelty to animals, when he felt emotionally rejected by his mother. He felt the need to externalize his pain and watch vulnerable creatures suffer.

Any schoolmates who even slightly offended him bore the brunt of the most intense vindictiveness – not directly to their face – but in the form of letting down the tyres on their bikes or defacing their schoolwork.

Marvin's main target for blame for what he is, is his mother, who he claims never gave him any love and affection as a child. He felt that his mother didn't really like him, and preferred his sister. The main influence on his upbringing was his grandmother. All his life he has carried with him an overwhelming sense of emotional rejection. He then projects this deep-rooted anguish on to his wife who he subconsciously punishes for what he believes he suffered as a child.

Marvin is totally negative in every respect – seeing the downside to every aspect of life – "his cup is half empty, not half full".

To his wife in particular, who he has chosen to bear the brunt of his extremely dangerous personality, he perpetuates "the dripping tap" of emotional abuse, continually focusing on the bad things in her life – mainly caused by him, and playing them to their maximum advantage. The more upset she becomes the more he does it.

Marvin has a very bad temper and functions on a short fuse. If members of his family don't do what he wants he can become very violent. If a small household chore becomes frustrating, he can fly into a terrible rage.

All in all, Marvin is a seriously damaged personality who may possibly have faulty "brain wiring" which prevents him from having any form of conscience or being able to feel compassion or remorse. He has an overwhelming "compulsion to repeat" – to inflict on other people the suffering he experienced as a child, using his most feared weapons, the withdrawal of love and emotional rejection, combined with humiliation and degradation, against other people.

Contrary to popular belief psychopaths are not all vicious serial killers. It is believed that around 1 in 200 people has strong psychopathic traits and many psychopathic individuals are found in big business. Their traits of ruthlessness, charm and callousness are valuable in manipulating their colleagues and opposing business interests.

~   ~   ~

Another feature of the psychopath is the paedophile.

Paedophilia appears to be a very deeply ingrained personality defect, and paedophiles are either psychopaths or have extremely strong psychopathic traits. Invariably they can see nothing wrong with their behaviour and it is not uncommon for them to refer to Freud's concept of "childhood sensuality" as an excuse for their crimes.

**The fact of the matter is that children do not
have sexual feelings in the sense that an
adult would understand them.**

"The Worthing Herald" recently carried news reports of two paedophile court cases. In one report the trial judge described a child rapist as "a compulsive and promiscuous paedophile". This man preyed on the young and vulnerable – children as young as 9 years old, and had devastated the lives of his victims. He raped and sexually abused children over a period of several years, "grooming" his victims by befriending them and then threatening them with violence.

It was only recently that this man, after having had continuous and intensive psychotherapy, had come to perceive himself as an abuser, **previously seeing himself as a victim.**

In another report, members of a violent paedophile ring were sentenced for crimes against girls aged between 8 and 13 years old. *"They showed no emotion as their sentences were imposed"*.

~   ~   ~

Mental cruelty and emotional abuse

"Emotional Power Games" are often based on a sense of inferiority, possibly as a result of being a younger child, or the youngest child in the family.

Emotional Vampirism is a particularly unpleasant form of mental cruelty and involves a victim being kicked when they are down. Their partner will wait until they are at their weakest and most vulnerable and then go through their memory banks for some real or imagined injustice in the past and then go for "payback". This is not only vicious but extremely cowardly.

Emotional abuse can also take the form of verbal attack and people will remember emotionally disturbing verbal abuse for a long time.

I carried out an experiment (using a sample of 20 mature students) into the effects of highly emotionally charged language and its ability to be retained in our memories.

When given two differently worded descriptions of the same event, one using a strong emotional language and the other using neutral language, these people rapidly absorbed the emotional language, repeated it word for word and could remember it for several days afterwards. This would indicate that it went straight into their long term memories. Harsh words make a dramatic impact and are remembered.

~   ~   ~

The mentally and emotionally cruel person is a coward. They use their most feared weapon against other people i.e. they inflict on others what would hurt them the most. This is part of the "compulsion to repeat" – where people have an overwhelming compulsion to inflict on others their own destructive childhood experiences.

~   ~   ~

MIND GAMES

"Why should marriage bring only tears?
All I wanted was a man
With a single heart
And we would stay together
As our hair turned white
Not somebody always after wriggling fish
With his big bamboo rod."

Chuo Wën-Chün
Chinese poet

Parent/adult/child ways of functioning

Eric Berne, stated:

> **emotionally damaged people play games and that the**
> **more damaged they are the more intensely**
> **they play them**.

He described various situations whereby people take on rôles for the purpose of pursuing their own ends. Particularly in relation to personal relationships he described "Marital Games" and "Sexual Games" whereby a person adopts a strategy for meeting a deep-rooted psychological need.

In the game of "Look how hard I've tried", Berne describes the scenario of a man being told he has an ulcer but he chooses to keep it secret from his wife and friends.

He continues working hard and eventually collapses at work. His implicit message to her is supposed to be "Look how hard I am trying", but instead of feeling remorse for previous marital arguments and loving him more, her sole reason for staying with him will be guilt. This also creates in his wife a very serious sense of resentment, feeling trapped through duty. If he had to gain her love with some type of material possession, she could return it.

According to Eric Berne every person carries their parents inside themselves. Everyone has a functioning adult somewhere inside them. Everyone carries a small child (a little boy or small girl) around inside them.

With immature people the Adult is deeply hidden and it is the Child who is in control most of the time.

The child in us can provide intuition, creativity, spontaneity and enjoyment. The child cannot cope with adult problems and a good functioning Adult state is necessary for survival.

A good functioning Parent is essential for dealing automatically, confidently and easily with important decisions.

All of these ego states are produced by person's upbringing.

Often one party is in the Child mode and the other is in the Parent mode and this can be the norm for a lot of marital relationships. One party is grown-up and responsible and makes all the decisions, whilst the other party is passive and dependent and needs to be told what to do.

Problems arise when one partner initiates a conversation from an Adult mode and expects an Adult response, but instead gets a response which is more appropriate to Parent-Child interaction.

Judy is concerned about Jeremy's drinking.

> In an Adult-Adult conversation Judy would express her concern to Jeremy that his drinking is damaging his health and draining the household budget. Jeremy would verbally acknowledge her communication, accept that she has made a valid point and offer to some sort of commitment for positive change.

When we are interacting with our partners or our families good methods of communication are absolutely essential.

When two people are functioning on an Adult level there is no problem.

An Adult level of functioning produces clear and emotionally mature information exchanges.

In this type of exchange there is good quality communication and a mature attitude on both sides.

> In an unsatisfactory exchange Judy would approach Jeremy about his drinking as an adult. Jeremy then complains that Judy is always nagging and that in his opinion, she has worse faults than he does. He then pressurizes her into stating exact dates, times and places when he has drunk too much and how much he has drunk and then challenges her to prove it.
>
> Instead of responding as an adult, Jeremy takes on a Child mode (naughty boy) and treats Judy as a scolding mother (punishing parent). Therefore what should be an adult-adult communication, in fact is a parent-child one which creates intense anger in Judy.

~   ~   ~

Eric Berne described the game of "The Frigid Woman".

The husband makes sexual advances to his wife but he is repulsed. She finds an excuse, for example, that he doesn't love her or all that he is interested in is sex. After a length of time has elapsed, she may walk into the bedroom half-dressed or even naked. She may also flirt with other men. The husband may then try to make sexual overtures to his wife again and again be rejected. Berne then describes the game of "Uproar" occurring as a direct result of everything which has gone on previously. In the game of "Uproar" the recent behaviour and other unrelated issues are argued about, the altercation being terminated by a door being slammed.

Berne thought that instead of the grievance being resolved by sexual activity "Uproar" is a substitute for the sexual act itself.

Berne also described the game "If it weren't for you" where a woman marries a dominating man so he will restrict her activities and thus keep her from getting into situations which frighten her.

Instead of being grateful for this she complains about restrictions he puts on her. This is easy for her to cope with as she can blame her husband for her own shortcomings.
This is a feature of the inferiority complex.

⁓   ⁓   ⁓

Bill and Janet have been married for five years, and what was origi-nally an intense sexual attraction has now petered out into a rather monotonous co-existence.

Janet is extremely dissatisfied with the state of the marriage, and is extremely concerned about the fact that Bill appears to be "working late" on a regular basis.

Janet approaches Bill about their lack of joint activities and a virtually non-existent sex life.

Janet: *"Bill, have you got a minute?*

     I'd like to talk about our marriage".

Bill: *"I'm watching this programme on TV at the moment".*

Janet*: "You seem to be working late a lot these days".*

Bill*: "Have you got a problem with that?"*

Janet*: "I thought it would be nice to spend more time together".*

Bill: *"We do, don't we?"*

Janet*: "You always seem pre-occupied".*

Bill: *"When? You tell me when I been pre-occupied".*

Janet*: "Well it seems all the time now".*

Bill: *"What do you think I'm pre-occupied about?"*

Janet: *"I would like you to tell me".*

Bill: *"What gives you the impression I'm pre-occupied?"*

Janet: *"Well, I speak to you and you don't answer."*

Bill: *"You do that, don't you?"*

Janet*: "But I'm talking about you."*

Bill: *"Why do you keep asking me questions?"*

Janet*: "I'm trying to get to the bottom of what's wrong with you."*

Bill: *"You're always looking for trouble."*

~   ~   ~

Eddie has been spending a lot of money on alcohol and gambling and apart from finding receipts for bottles of whisky and betting slips it is evident to Karen, Eddie's partner, that he has been drinking heavily over a long period of time and gambling away the mortgage money.

Eddie knows that Karen knows what he's doing. Karen knows that Eddie knows that she knows what he is doing.

He refuses to admit his behaviour, even in the face of the evidence. So who is he trying to deceive – only himself. Does he really expect Karen to believe his lies and denials when she has clear evidence of his activities?

~   ~   ~

Carol is the mother of two children. She is preoccupied with problems surrounding the death of her father. Her husband, in order to conceal his bad behaviour and to gain the loyalty of his children, poisons their minds against their mother by making false allegations about her personal integrity.

She has a vague awareness of this but her husband refuses to admit to what he's doing. This creates in Carol intense feelings of paranoia.

~   ~   ~

Jack is behaving strangely – probably because he has been up to no good. Jill reacts by being profoundly irritated by his behaviour.

Jack reacts to Jill's irritation by becoming hostile; refusing to acknowledge the cause of Jill's annoyance.

There is deadlock and someone has to back down.

Jack refuses to back down as he will then have to admit to having committed a wrongdoing – his behaviour being his protection against Jill's anger.

Jill backs down, when in fact she has done no wrong; a woman's place usually being in the wrong.

~   ~   ~

The "Vicious Circle"

I've done you wrong and you've complained
and so I'll do you even more wrong

Joe is a liar and a troublemaker. Instead of being ashamed of what he is, he is proud of it. He feels it gives him some type of status in the world. He sees himself as a Don Juan – a ladies' man – a geezer. In fact other people see him as a sad idiot.

He believes he has a very charming side to his personality, combined with a projection of vulnerability which makes him attractive to women. Underneath this, however, lies a viciousness which comes to the fore if anyone upsets Joe. He is emotionally hypersensitive and cannot cope with either criticism or confrontation.

Jenny has had a long-term relationship with Joe and out of a misguided sense of loyalty has stuck with him. It is only recently that Jenny has realized that the problems in the relationship are not her fault.

A long-standing and predictable pattern of behaviour is that Joe does something wrong, Jenny complains about it which offends Joe as he does not cope well with confrontation. Joe then retaliates to Jenny's complaint about his behaviour by doing something vindictive behind her back. Jenny finds out about his misdemeanours and complains again, which again prompts Joe into an act of vindictiveness. It is a vicious circle of abuse which is instigated purely by Joe who expects to be forgiven for anything he does, but cannot in fact forgive Jenny for complaining. If she ignores him, he finds that unacceptable; if she complains he finds that unacceptable.

Joe needs to learn that if he offends and upsets then he should "take it on the nose" and offer Jenny some form of compensation for the distress he has caused her. Joe expects to go through life doing what he wants to other people without any "comeback".

Joe is the centre of his own universe. Everyone else is always wrong and he is always right. If people disagree with him or pick fault with him then they have something wrong with them.

Immaturity is a dominant feature of Joe's personality, and it is an extension of the underlying high anxiety levels caused by his wrongdoing.

Jenny has, for many years, complained to Joe about his poor lovemaking techniques. Joe, however, demands that Jenny provides him with skilled sexual techniques even when she is ill, tired, or just not in the mood. Everything has to come from Jenny, and Joe sits back and criticizes her whilst making no effort himself.

Joe's main weapon is vindictiveness. At even the slightest affront Joe goes on "payback" big-time and when Jenny objects he retaliates with more vindictiveness, so a vicious circle of misery is created.

Joe is the anal personality type. Joe also has an inferiority complex – projecting his shortcomings and insecurities on to Jenny. He is vicious – he sticks the knife in and turns it slowly.

Joe is suspicious of Jenny – because he cheats on Jenny he mistrusts her. When Jenny questions him about his suspicious behaviour he accuses her of being paranoid.

In fact, it is actually Joe who is paranoid. Because of his involvement with other women Joe is continually looking over his shoulder for angry husbands tracking him down.

Joe blames everyone and everything for his own inadequacies. He assumes every conversation involves people making derogatory comments about him, and he transfers all his faults and negative perceptions on to other people.

～　　　～　　　～

The Martyr

Malcolm is extremely emotionally insecure and is very quick to take very severe offence at the slightest form of criticism. The main feature of his personality is self-pity and an overwhelming sense of inferiority.

Whatever Malcolm does wrong in his life – he blames someone or something else for his misdeeds. He refuses point blank to take any responsibility whatsoever for anything he has done wrong – he blames his upbringing, work stress, alcohol, his wife, his age, the children and even the dog.

Malcolm's wife feels extremely dissatisfied with the state of the marriage as Malcolm continually does her wrong either by word (upsetting her with ill-conceived remarks) or deed (being unfaithful, selfish and overcritical of her).

Malcolm actually creates situations he can martyr himself in. He won't ever take the easy way to do things but has to do a job in a way that involves the most effort, the most inconvenience and of course the most martyrdom.

Malcolm expects instant forgiveness for anything he may have done wrong and feels extremely sorry for himself – even if his mistake has damaged his wife. If his wife commits even the most trivial mistake, he punishes her relentlessly. He is weak and cannot face responsibility. When his wife is upset about something he can only offer some type of comfort to her provided she can produce a reason for her distress that does not blame him. If she blames him for upsetting her, then he feels sorry for himself.

Malcolm has lost his job on a couple of occasions because of bad conduct – he blames preoccupation with his marriage problems on this.

Malcolm has what is known as the "oral personality type", as described by Freud and this is rooted in the first two years of childhood. Malcolm's mother had problems feeding Malcolm at the breast and had another baby very shortly afterwards which pushed him out.

Malcolm is very emotionally intense and sees everything on an emotional level, very seldom giving problems or situations an intellectual input. He has mood swings and spends a lot of time daydreaming and fantasising. He is a heavy smoker and is prone to depression and "compulsive behaviour" having no control over a lot of his behaviour.

The Big Kid

The main feature of the Big Kid's personality is that he reacts against his wife as though she is his mother.

Roy is extremely immature. He functions on the lowest moral level, which is fear of punishment, having the mentality of a "naughty boy". He knows the difference between right and wrong but chooses not to exercise it. Although he is in his 40's he is still rather like a rebellious teenager. He is still reacting against his parents and their values, and reacts against his wife as though she holds parental power.

Roy's only driving force in life is self- gratification and self-protection. He can be almost infantile in his behaviour towards his wife. He often waits until she is preoccupied with tasks to do, or problems to solve, but instead of helping, he uses this as an opportunity to do wrong, knowing that his chances of detection are reduced.

Roy will also use the fact that his wife is unhappy for some reason to go on "payback", using any small mistake she may have made, however long ago, as an excuse to victimize her when she is at her weakest. He neglects ever to take any of his behaviour into account. Roy also uses "cryptic clues" in communicating with his wife – he will put on music or a film which obviously has some relevance to an existing domestic situation and uses this medium to communicate his sentiments regarding the ongoing problem.

Roy is too immature to communicate directly with his wife – he confesses to misdemeanours in company and then denies them later. For this reason alone their relationship is tenuous.

Roy's behaviour is totally negative and undesirable – he actually feels self-loathing. He has very low self-esteem, created by childhood experiences. He has felt suicidal on several occasions.

Roy also deliberately attempts to destroy his wife's self-confidence in the belief that by doing so she will not leave him for someone else – someone who he feels will be better than him.

Roy's behaviour has strong elements of the childhood emotions felt towards his mother, when he felt he was not particularly favoured by her. He believes she failed to give him sufficient attention, and is punishing his wife for his mother's perceived shortcomings.

Roy is both devious and a coward.

~   ~   ~

The Psychiatrist

"You are mental"

Peter has been persistently unfaithful to Ann throughout the course of their marriage. He is weak and unable to resist temptation and feels that one woman isn't enough for him. His problems are rooted in childhood where he felt neglected by his mother who was always too busy to pay much attention to him.

However, although Peter realizes he has a problem, he refuses to get help for it, even to the extent he will not admit his "dalliances" to Ann – even when presented with the evidence.

Ann has always had doubts about Peter's fidelity, but increasingly during the period of the marriage she finds concrete evidence relating to his extramarital relationships. Peter's ruse is to claim that Ann is mentally ill – paranoid – in constantly accusing him of affairs.

Ann is incensed by Peter's attitude and behaviour. She is degraded by his infidelity and insulted by the fact that he constantly requests that **she** should see a Psychiatrist because she is unable to trust him.

Peter persists in his strategy with Ann as a form of self-protection for himself – he watches her for any slight evidence of emotional distress, nervousness, or irritability which is caused by his bad behaviour, and then suggests she seek professional help for her "problem".

He also cites her failure to believe his obviously transparent lies as even more evidence of her "mental illness".

Peter also suffers from "selective memory syndrome" in that he appears not to be able to remember things he's done wrong in the past – again citing Ann's "mental illness" as the cause of her "deranged" perception of previous events.

Peter himself is actually suffering from a personality disorder with strong psychopathic traits. He will achieve self-gratification at all costs, show no remorse or compassion for those he is hurting, and will seek only to protect himself with any mechanism he can find.

~   ~   ~

Adultery

It is the emotional and spiritual, as well as the intellectual aspects of the personality, which keep a tight rein on the strong desires of the libido (the life force expressed through the sex drive).

The superego (which is produced by paternal authority) should be civilising as well as restraining. Good maternal nurturing produces conscience – the desire for sexual gratification is there but the restraints are put into place.

A combination of intelligent joint parenting should remove the desire for the compulsive satisfaction of instinctive needs.

Alice Miller described a patient who repeatedly, to the point of obsession, seduced women and then abandoned them. She believed that he experienced feelings of helplessness, jealousy and loneliness as a small child and that these emotions were produced by an "unresolved Oedipus Complex"; that fear of castration he felt as a small boy for desiring his mother remained with him into adulthood.

This man, during analysis, was able to recall the experience of being repeatedly abandoned by his mother. It was not until he actually had children of his own that he could acknowledge the intense emotions he had felt so early in his life.

It is possible that many men are compulsive womanizers in order to fend off strong homosexual impulses. It is almost as if they are trying to prove to themselves and other people that they are heterosexual. I believe these men to be in doubt about their masculinity.

If the Oedipus Complex is not successfully resolved by identification with the father, then the boy will give up all hope of being a man, will identify with the mother and subconsciously offer himself to the father as a sexual object.

There is also the phenomenon of "ultra-feminine" women – adults who dress themselves in frilly clothes and need to constantly have the attention of men.

This can be related to an unresolved "Electra Complex", where the girl's strongest attachment is to her father.

The adulterer makes himself feel better about what he is doing by continually picking fault with the person he is cheating on. He may focus his attention on domestic trivia, his wife's clothing or hairstyle or generally be irritable and aggressive with her and other people in general.

Adulterers live in fear of discovery and this makes them feel insecure. They then become suspicious of their partners.

Often adultery is purely an act of maliciousness on the part of the adulterer. They may deliberately go out and sleep with someone to take revenge on a partner for a perceived injustice.

> Les had a promising career in a rock band when he met Estelle. He was instantly sexually attracted and within months Estelle was pregnant. Because Estelle came from a very strictly religious family, abortion was out of the question. According to her family's wishes they got married, but the marriage was fraught with all types of tensions. Les had to get a "mainstream" job to support his wife and child. Their

many problems, which include financial ones, are compounded by the fact that Les's in-laws neither like nor approve of him.

One particular evening they are invited to a wedding reception, but Estelle chooses the early part of the evening to have the local vicar to the house to organize their baby's christening. Les goes to the wedding and has sex with a young woman there, purely and simply as an act of revenge against Estelle for becoming pregnant and forcing on him an undesirable lifestyle.

Adultery can be an act of defiance against what is perceived to be a domineering partner.

Richard was always rather weak and indecisive. This is a result of lack of confidence and he never trusts his judgment on any important matters. He feels more comfortable in seeking out the opinion of his wife, Christine, who is intelligent and self-assured and is trusted for her sound judgment.

However Richard feels that Christine's confidence can border on arrogance. This is, however, not necessarily true. Richard has a rather distorted perspective on what is assertive and what is aggressive. The same is true regarding his perceptions of the difference between confidence and arrogance. This is the main stumbling block of the marriage.

Richard often feels his masculinity is under threat by the fact that Christine takes all the major decisions in their life together. He feels that, although he never voices an opinion, Christine is domineering.

The fact of the matter is that it always has to be Christine who has had to deal with all the problems, particularly of those with banks, schools, etc as Richard lacks the confidence and verbal ability to cope with matters like these.

Richard has an over-developed sense of self-pity, looking only at his own feelings and has very little sympathy for anybody else.

He is actively looking for a "girlie" type woman who is passive, lacking in confidence, unintelligent and vulnerable – someone who will be impressed with the few positive qualities he has. He wants someone to look up to him – something which Christine is unable to do.

Richard picks up with Mandy, many years his junior. Mandy is pretty, feminine, gullible, and compliant and looks up to Richard despite his numerous faults. Mandy is impressed with Richard's strategies to impress her and she rewards him for what he gives her materially and financially with totally uninhibited sexual behaviour – agreeing to do everything Richard asks her to do in bed.

UNDERSTANDING DESTRUCTIVE
FAMILY RELATIONSHIPS

UPBRINGING

"These are thy glorious works, Parent of good…"

John Milton

Mother Love

"She is very touching in her sweet little marks of affection ... when I have seemed unhappy about little things she has come and held up her sweet mouth to be kissed... How very precious may the remembrance of them become"

Elizabeth Gaskell

The most basic human need is a sense of security. This is formed in infancy by the bonding of mother and child through love and its associations with nourishment and protection.

Alice Miller claimed that the type of emotional atmosphere surrounding a child's first year of life is crucial for a sense of security.

"Maternal warmth and body contact of are of irreplaceable value for the child's later development"

The Psychologists, Harry and Margaret Harlow, worked with infant monkeys to find out whether early experiences of being mothered had a lasting effect on their emotional development and affected their ability to be good mothers themselves.

The Harlows built two substitute mothers:

> ❖ a bare wire-frame "mother" with a feeding bottle containing milk attached to it

> ❖ a cloth "mother" offering comfort, but no food

They found that the infant monkeys preferred the "cloth mother" even though it did not offer food: the "emotional warmth" provided by the physical comfort was preferred.

These infant monkeys raised with the substitute mothers made poor mothers themselves later in life as they had no direct experience of all the things a mother could give: love, comfort, grooming and good quality interaction.

The research seems to show that there is not necessarily a concept called "maternal instinct" and that good mothering is learned from direct experience.

The Jesuits stated:

"Give us the child and we will show you the man"

Freud believed:

"The child is father to the man"

According to Freud our first experience of love is with our parents, particularly our mothers, and all future relationships are thought to be based on this foundation.

**Being loved either by a parent or a partner gives
a person a sense of worth.**

Some people who don't feel valued on a personal level may compensate themselves with material wealth and possessions.

Parents have to be both nurturing and punishing and the voice of authority, setting the rules for behaviour.

The first five years of life are believed to be the most formative and the experiences a child has during this time are thought to be instrumental in forming the adult personality.

A child's personality traits are believed to be completely formed by the age of eight years.

Maternal Deprivation

Alice Miller believes that:

> **the repression of our suffering destroys our**
> **ability to relate to the suffering of others.**

❖ parents who have never known love are unable to give love. On their coming into the world they were met with coldness, insensitivity and indifference.

❖ formerly abused children often say, "That's the way I was brought up and I turned out all right – that's how I'll bring up my children too".

An ulcer can form if a person has a repressed and unfulfilled childhood longing for parental love: by continually producing acid, the stomach is preparing itself for food, which is a symbol for love.

People who appear to have survived childhood abuse have probably recognized early in their lives that their parents' behaviour is severely abnormal and form emotional attachments with other adults, for example their teachers or other relatives.

~   ~   ~

THE ONCE SILENCED CHILD IN US NEEDS TO BE ABLE
TO FEEL AND SPEAK

The adverse effects experienced by an infant when separated from the mother are called **"Maternal Deprivation"**.

Research carried out in the 1940s and 1950s by John Bowlby revealed that juvenile thieves had suffered long separations from their mothers at crucial stages in their lives.

The first year of life is the most important for
forming bonds of love and affection.

The effects of the separation caused severe distress up until the age of three. These children, even those who were separated even for just a few weeks, grew up to be emotionally disturbed.

This promoted the belief that the uninterrupted presence of a mother was essential for a child's normal psychological development. This gave rise to the notion that:

if you don't do five years "hard labour" when
the child is young, then you will have to do it
later.

This created tremendous pressure on mothers in the 1950s to direct their energies into the home and family and ignored the benefits of good quality childcare and nursery provision.

John Bowlby considered that Mother Love in infancy was as important for mental health as vitamins and proteins are for physical health.

~   ~   ~

Although "Maternal Deprivation" is believed to occur when an infant is separated physically from the mother, is has also been observed to happen when the child is in the continuous care of the mother.

Researchers studied a pair of twins whose father had left home soon after their birth. The mother was loving and affectionate towards her daughter, but she was cold and rejecting towards her son, even though he was clean, well-fed and well-dressed.

The physical growth of the emotionally deprived boy became stunted. The loved daughter grew normally, but her twin brother at age 13 months was only the size of an 8 month old child.

Sir Michael Rutter claimed that children who suffer separation from their mothers in the first year of life are likely to be psychologically damaged and have difficulty in forming close friendships and sexual relationships in adulthood.

Failure to form bonds of affection during infancy could create a psychopathic personality, where an affectionless and brutal personality, incapable of remorse, is disguised by an aura of being a nice person.

Research has shown that antisocial children, who survived into middle life and didn't die from accidents, suicide or alcoholism, did eventually become more responsible conforming adults, giving credence to the idea that some allegedly antisocial psychopaths can "come right".

Even "normal" babies in loving families benefit immensely from being talked to and played with. Apart from stimulating their social development it creates the opportunity for them to learn complex speech patterns, and to develop a good vocabulary. Good quality interaction with babies and toddlers also promotes intellectual development and reasoning ability.

Babies and toddlers offered conversation, stimulation and close loving contact are more likely to grow to be well-adjusted than children who only have their immediate physical needs met.

Research carried out by the American Association for the Advancement of Science in 2006 confirmed that depriving children of a loving family environment causes lasting damage not only to their emotional well-being but also to their intelligence and physical growth.

~   ~   ~

Alice Miller believes that children who are allowed to express anger in an acceptable way, will grow up to be stable adults and react to grievances verbally, instead of lashing out.

Small children:

  ❖ **are hurt and wounded**

  ❖ **risk losing their parent's love and affection if they express their anger**

  ❖ **store up their anger**
      discharging it on others later in life
      direct it inwardly – possibly self-harming.

She believes the child's anger is healthy and represents a source of vitality.

Children who are made to repress their anger may grow into adults who are:

❖ suicidal

❖ drug addicts.

She believes drug addicts are seeking their true selves, but actually they are punishing themselves for doing this. They are destroying their own spontaneous feelings and vitality, repeating the experience of being punished during childhood.

She relates the story of a patient of hers who had been treated in a very cruel way by his father. They both shared the same delusion that what the patient received as a child was "discipline", and he was very grateful to his father for his strict upbringing and the "severe punishments" he had received. However the patient also had "severe symptoms". Only as he got older did he realize his father was:

❖ repeating on him what he had himself experienced as a child

❖ continually hurting his feelings by either ignoring him or ridiculing him.

The patient's father truly believed that he was preparing his son for the outside world by the way he treated him and that he should be thanked for his efforts.
A child is often used as a substitute for one's own parents. Adults often pin their own hang-ups on their children and use them as a scapegoat for what they have experienced as children.

There is often behaviour which reflects:

❖ An unconscious need to pass on to others the humiliation and pain they experienced

❖ The child becoming an object to manipulate.

These children can be subjected to many contradictory wishes and expectations they often cannot meet. This can in extreme cases create psychosis, drug addiction or the person can be driven to suicide.

False beliefs about child-rearing:

❖ Love is produced from a sense of duty

❖ Parents deserve respect without earning it

❖ Obedience is character forming

❖ High self-esteem is harmful to development.

The deliberate use of humiliation of a child to compensate the parent or other adult (such as a relative or a teacher) destroys the child's self-confidence making them insecure and inhibited.

≈   ≈   ≈

Childhood perspectives

People tend to carry their childhood experiences through to adulthood.

Eric Berne described "The Sulk" who is angry with his mother and has been angry with her since early childhood as a direct result of some disturbing or traumatising experience.

He does not like women although he may be a Don Juan.
Female "Sulks" are angry at their fathers for similar reasons.

Bad childhood experiences often remain dormant until there is a catalyst – often a family bereavement – which can open up a Pandora's box of pent-up emotion. This can relate to brothers and sisters having very different perspectives on their upbringing depending on their positions in the family.

They may perceive that the way they were treated as children was based purely on their merits as a person.

The actual situation is usually related to the existing family circumstances.

- ❖ workplace stress

- ❖ the state of the parents' marriage

- ❖ financial considerations

- ❖ problems with other family members.

Adults may have gone through several decades of life truly believing that the way their parents treated them related solely to their personal qualities.

~   ~   ~

Alice Miller claims that a child may be very damaged by being forced to love what does not deserve to be loved. This is often the case when a child is being sexually abused by a family member.

A child may even accept sexual abuse for the sake of finding at least some affection rather than freezing up entirely. She believes that with a loving, protective, perceptive and courageous mother, a child cannot be abused.

Alice Miller states that:

all people who abuse children were themselves abused as children.

This is a result of the compulsion to repeat.

She considers that crucial to a child's healthy emotional development is that they receive respect from their parents and other caregivers, that their emotional needs are met and that there is tolerance for their feelings.

Childhood sexual abuse is extremely psychologically damaging. The way a victim's complaints are dealt with is crucial in determining the extent of the emotional disturbance the child will suffer.

~ ~ ~

Greg is a nice guy but shy and retiring with a sexual repressed upbringing. He is rather a loner and has a lot of vague anxieties which make him feel generally ill at ease with life and generally uncomfortable with himself. He feels, and has done for most of his adult life, to be "shell-shocked" but cannot quite put his finger on the cause of it.

Greg does remember, however, that as a boy some other boys he knew very well "dragged him into a shed and put straw down his back". After that incident he was unable to remember what they looked like. When he was relating his story Greg showed very strong signs of some traumatic memory which he couldn't quite bring to consciousness.

It is obvious from Greg's recollection of events that these boys did a lot more than put straw down his back.

Greg is suffering from traumatic amnesia. This is a condition where profoundly emotionally distressing events are blocked out from consciousness and the person has no memory of the trauma. However, the trauma damages the personality and psychological health of the sufferer and they often become plagued by anxieties and phobias they don't understand.

~   ~   ~

Joanna was sexually abused by a male friend of the family as an 11-year-old child in the late 1930s.

"I used to like going to his house and playing with his dog, which he encouraged. I loved that dog and we had a lot of fun together. After a while he started sitting me on his lap and talking about his dog with me and then he would put his hand inside my knickers. I felt very uncomfortable about this. I went home and told my mother. She was quite flippant about it and just said I shouldn't go over there any more".

~   ~   ~

Josephine is 10 years old: she is happy and intelligent. She is top of the class and her teacher – Mr Jones – treats her as his favourite.

Mr Jones asks Josephine to help out with preparing work for the less able children, something that makes Josephine feel special. She is relishing how clever she is and how important this makes her feel. At one point when they are alone together, Mr Jones puts his hands inside Josephine's knickers and strokes her genitals. Josephine feels a sense of some form of sexual awakening – an exaggerated form of what she has felt for boys of the same age, but this is combined with an overwhelming sense of shock, disgust, fear and outrage.

Josephine is terrified – the physical sensations of sexuality have been transformed into terror which then encompasses her body – the mixture of fear and sexual arousal causes large amounts of adrenaline to pump through her body and her young mind struggles to understand what is happening to her. Who does she tell? She is frightened that if it becomes public will be branded as a troublemaker and victimized by other children. She is terrified that her father will find out as she knows he will be violent towards Mr Jones.

Josephine decides to say nothing. She carries around with her an enormous sense of guilt and becomes very depressed. She starts to suffer from repeated headaches which prevent her from going to school. She still feels "special", but in a negative way. She wonders why Mr Jones has singled her out from the other children for the gratification of his sexual needs. She feels dirty, degraded and paranoid. She believes that other children and their parents "know" what has been done to her and that she will not be welcome in their homes because she is "unclean".

Within a short period of time another pupil complains to her parents about Mr Jones's behaviour and the police are brought in. This then unleashes a flood of complaints from other parents whose children have been abused by Mr Jones. It appears that Mr Jones has been abusing children on a regular basis over a long period of time and Josephine is just one of many.

~   ~   ~

Failure to provide a child with emotional security can create a damaged adult personality, particularly if this child's genetic makeup is one of extreme emotional sensitivity. A more resilient child may be able to withstand a more adverse start to life.

At one end of the spectrum, failure to receive good nurturing can be compensated for by a need for money and material possessions as a source of security – at the other extreme mental illness can be created.

Alice Miller relates the story of one of her patients who, from a very young age, was trained to ignore hunger pains and his parents took his mind off these by giving him affection. As an adult he developed a set of complicated compulsive symptoms which stemmed from deep feelings of insecurity.

She believes that if badly treated children are not to become criminal or mentally ill, it is essential that at least once in their life they have contact with someone who can recognize that it is the environment not the "poor wretched child" that is to blame.

Here the influence of inherited personality traits comes into force. Children with strong personalities are likely to have some degree of resilience to bad parenting. Children with weak personalities will be over-sensitive to any mistakes their parents make, however well intentioned.

Alice Miller comments on the fact that impartial observers raise the objection to the power of bad parenting to damage a child by comparing people who had difficult childhoods and who grew up without obvious ill-effects with people who had favourable home conditions and who grew up to be mentally ill.

The researcher, Avshalom Caspi, has studied males who were mistreated as children. Some of them grew up to become violent but others with a different inherited brain chemistry proved to have coped with their bad treatment and were not violent as adults.

~   ~   ~

Parenting styles

Some very important ingredients in managing a child's behaviour have been found by Psychologists:

❖ developing bonds of mutual love and respect between the parents and children

❖ being consistent in setting rules and limits on behaviour
❖ providing good quality rôle models for behaviour

❖ using reasoning in discipline

❖ giving children and adolescents responsibility.

Withdrawing privileges is more effective than physical punishment. The problem with "conventional" methods of discipline, such as grounding, is that the child may decide to "do the crime and do the time" – knowing what the punishment will be, the child can decide whether the enjoyment they will get from the "forbidden" activity will be worth the sacrifice made with the privilege withdrawn.

An effective method of using the withdrawal of privileges to its maximum benefit is threatening to refuse to grant the next thing the child will ask for – a totally unknown quantity. Most children will imagine some profoundly pleasurable activity being denied to them and usually comply with their parents requests.

Rewarding good behaviour is also very effective but continually giving a reward immediately after good behaviour can become predictable and "extinguished". An effective way of rewarding good behaviour is to give rewards "out of the blue" for long periods of good behaviour, often when the child least expects it – this is very reinforcing.

~   ~   ~

The rôle of fathers in childrearing cannot be ignored and it has been a consistent theme, when looking at "bad families", that the blame for problems is placed totally on the mothers.

Obviously the presence of two caring parents is the ideal.

Fathers tend to have a more physical relationship with their children – playing games of rough and tumble, whilst mothers are more "intellectual" – talking and reading.

Research carried out in the 1960s by Psychologists Rudolf Schaffer and Peggy Emerson in Glasgow, Scotland showed that nearly one third of 18 month old children were most strongly attached to their fathers.

The rôle of fatherhood in parental styles of discipline is very important, as in some families the discipline of children is considered to be the father's responsibility.

- ❖ **Permissiveness:** the parents allow the child free rein to do what they want to do with few restrictions on behaviour. These children are not particularly happy or well-behaved.

- ❖ **Democratic:** the parents take the child's views into consideration and make the final decision about important issues. The children brought up by this method tend to be well adjusted.

- ❖ **Authoritarian:** the parents are very strict, allow no dissent and reserve the right to rule the child completely. They exercise rigid control over their children. Their children tend to break the rules as soon as their parent's backs are turned.

~   ~   ~

Pressures on women

You can't kill the spirit
She is like a mountain
She's old and strong
She goes on and on.

There is no such thing as a perfect mother and many people grow up with a strong conflict between their idea of the perfect mother and the reality of a woman who is their mother – with both positive and negative qualities. Many people fantasize about the mother they would have liked. Women have the pressure of combining work with motherhood in a climate of child unfriendly workplaces and "work" unfriendly schools.

~   ~   ~

Many people blame feminism for the breakdown of the family unit. However, prior to the women's movement many women, particularly those who were married, were deeply unhappy, confused, frustrated, depressed and often self harming. All of these destructive emotions were detrimental both to the woman herself and to her family unit.

Again it is the case of a woman being blamed. Very many partnerships and marriages end because the man walks out of the family home, often leaving for a new and younger partner.

It is only in the last couple of decades that rape in marriage has been made illegal: prior to that was the concept of "conjugal rights" where a husband acquired ownership of his wife's body as a sexual unit at marriage.

The relaxed divorce laws of 1971 opened a "floodgate" of divorce petitions. Prior to this, divorce was extremely difficult for the ordinary person as it was extremely complicated and expensive.

Notorious stories

Adolf Hitler

What constitutes a "good" childhood is open to debate. Alice Miller carried out an in-depth study of Adolf Hitler and observed that although he had a very brutal father, his mother loved her son very much and spoiled him.

She considers that spoiling, where "every wish is granted and he is showered with things he does not need" causes untold harm. Good mothering means being "open and sensitive to the child's true needs".

Many of Hitler's biographers claimed that he received too much love from his mother and as an adult he translated the adoration he had from his mother into a desire to be worshipped by the masses.

Alice Miller believes that for Hitler the persecution of Jews allowed him to take revenge on his father, who was tyrannical and thought to be half Jewish.

It is possible that he felt "unclean" at his father having "mixed blood", as "purification" of the German race in all areas, including Slavs, Poles, etc was a major theme of the Nazi regime.

The other significant concept relating to Nazi Germany was "Lebensraum" – "living space" and Alice Miller feels that this was an unconscious way of liberating his German mother from a persecuting and tyrannical husband. She claims the rôle of dictator gave Hitler the opportunity to be obeyed as he had to obey his father and that the concentration camp was an unconscious symbolism for the containment and repression of the child and all his emotional needs which are to be annihilated.

~   ~   ~

Mary Bell

Mary Bell was sentenced to life imprisonment in England in 1968 for the murder of two young children.

At school, Mary hit, scratched and kicked other children and was seen trying to choke three small girls in a playground. She was cruel to animals, wringing the necks of pigeons and trying to strangle a cat.

At the time of her arrest she told police that she liked hurting little things that can't defend themselves and that she would like to be a nurse because then she could stick needles into people and she would enjoy hurting them.

Mary Bell was rejected both emotionally and physically by her mother, who tried to kill her at least four times before she was given away as a three-year-old. It is believed that Mary's biological mother had strong sadistic tendencies and is thought to have worked as a dominatrix as a part-time job. It is likely that Mary would have inherited some of her mother's sadistic tendencies.

Obviously hated, scorned, rejected and abused as a child, Mary Bell had the compulsion to repeat these experiences by inflicting harm and suffering on other children and other vulnerable creatures. Both children and animals receive love and affection – which she did not – her overwhelming compulsion was to destroy.

～　　　　～　　　　～

Beverley Allitt

This young woman, who worked in a nursing capacity, attacked 36 children in her care in a British hospital. She was convicted of the murder of four children and harming nine others, injecting them with either insulin or potassium. Allitt enjoyed the excitement these crises caused and revelled in being the centre of attention when attempts to revive the children were made.

Allitt appeared, particularly to the parents of the sick children, to be kind, friendly and caring and was so popular with some of the parents that she became godmother to one of the children she had harmed.

In her personal life Allitt systematically abused the trust and friendship given to her by other people – again making herself popular with them. She particularly promoted her status as a victim when police inquiries regarding the events at the hospital were going on, then simultaneously committed acts of extreme malice towards them, and allowing other people to take the blame for all of her acts of viciousness.

It is considered that her actions were calculated but that she had no control over her impulses, which indicates strong psychopathic traits.

It is believed that her abnormal behaviour emerged at around puberty when she was noticed to display a marked change in her behaviour. Allitt, by her own admission, was a pathological liar and thought that telling lies made life more interesting.

Allitt's behaviour could be described as extreme attention-seeking. As a child she was quiet and obedient. It is thought that she only tended to receive love and attention when she hurt herself.

As a young adult she frequently presented herself at Casualty Departments at hospitals to receive attention to wounds caused by self-harming. She later obtained employment caring for sick children in a hospital.

It is likely that Allitt's behaviour was based on the compulsion to repeat, simultaneously identifying with the sick children, but at the same time having the impulse to destroy them – possibly a result of childhood suicidal thoughts. Undoubtedly the sick children in her care received a lot of attention, love and affection from their parents and the medical staff.

As a child she probably craved unconditional love from her parents and her sister. Her sister had a kitten of which Allitt was intensely jealous, claiming that her sister felt more for the kitten than she did for her. The kitten was later found with its head battered in.

Allitt was felt to have very low self-esteem and it is very likely that when she was seeking medical attention for physical wounds caused by self-harming, she was actually seeking help for emotional and psychological wounds perceived to have been caused by lack of love and affection.

Allitt was diagnosed as having Munchausen's Syndrome by Proxy – where the sufferer seeks to gain attention by creating sickness and injury in others.

~   ~   ~

The Krays

The Kray twins obviously displayed very strong psychopathic traits. Reggie, who was the 'straight' twin, was violent in a premeditated and controlled manner. Ronnie, the gay twin, was both emotionally volatile and violent – an explosive combination of the "female brain" and male testosterone. Interestingly when convicted for their crimes, Reggie was sent a conventional prison, whilst Ronnie was sent to Broadmoor, being declared criminally insane.

As children they were surrounded, loved and adored by strong-minded women, particularly their mother, Violet, who ran the business of being a family. No one ▓▓▓▓ with Violet's family.

The Krays' father was "ineffectual" – he was a petty thief and a weak character who appeared to have very little influence in his family.

The twins ran a "family business" – no one ▓▓▓▓ with the Krays. *"When people are afraid of you – you can do anything."*

As twins they had a very strong psychological and emotional bond – almost like a mental umbilical cord. [It has been my observation that often identical twins are "mirror images" of each other, almost like being separate components of the same personality].

As both Reggie and Ronnie had exactly the same upbringing it is likely that Ronnie's homosexuality was genetic. Although the family environment fitted the 'distant father/overprotective mother' scenario described by Freud, Reggie was straight. The twins obviously inherited their mother's strong personality traits and possibly felt a need to protect their mother from the outside world, in the absence of any strong male rôle model.

They were notoriously violent criminals, and as well as inflicting their brutality on other gangland members, "eliminated" anybody who stood in their way. The environment they lived in was very much like the "dog eat dog" world that business people inhabit, but in the Krays' world the backstabbing, cut-throat, shoot from the hip environment was literal and real.

~   ~   ~

BAD FAMILIES AND
PSYCHOLOGICAL DISORDER

"Throw away Thy rod
Throw away Thy wrath
O my God
Take the gentle path!"

George Herbert

Abnormal communication patterns

> *"Some atheist or vile infidel in love*
> *When I do speak of thy divinity*
> *May blaspheme and say I do flatter thee"*
>
> *Joshua Sylvester*

Abnormal communication patterns can be caused by the communicator either being devious or by them being psychologically disturbed. These communication patterns are profoundly destructive. I believe that three types of abnormal communication patterns are particularly damaging.

Blurred communication patterns

- ❖ Communicating through third parties in the presence of the target listener instead of directly to the person concerned

- ❖ Communicating through **deviousness**: making snide remarks in the presence of the target listener

- ❖ Dropping hints about misdemeanours in the presence of the target listener then denying it later when confronted

- ❖ Evasiveness – refusing to be "pinned down" about facts and situations.

In genuinely blurred communication patterns there is often a problem with conveying or articulating information.

This may be a result of:

- ❖ not wishing to hurt someone's feelings

- ❖ self protection.

In other types of blurred communication patterns the person is either unable or unwilling to understand the truth of the situation.

> William is homosexual. He had a very poor relationship with his father who he found to be hostile and rejecting towards him from an early age. He was always very much a Mummy's boy and she doted on him, particularly as he had a severe stammer, being the result of a brutal brand of fathering which started at age 4.

> As William gets older he begins to realize that he is homosexual, something which is confirmed at the age of 17 when he embarks on his first homosexual relationship.

> William claims that his mother is very demanding and controlling, using emotional blackmail to keep him as close to her as possible as her marriage is so bad. She has no idea that William is homosexual but his father has very strong suspicions.

> William is very self-centred and very self-absorbed and he has had treatment for a Narcissistic neurosis at the local hospital. He sees himself as the centre of the universe and expects other people to be as interested in him as he is in himself.

> William focuses his dissatisfaction with his life squarely on his mother's shoulders. Directly to her face and to other people, he claims that she is a burden on him and that without her his life would be completely different.

The older he gets the more he starts to resent his mother's emotional and psychological "engulfment" – the (s)mothering and feigning of illness when he wants his freedom. This increases dramatically after the death of his father when he and his mother find themselves living alone together.

William has frequent disputes with the neighbours and is generally considered to be a nuisance and a troublemaker amongst the people with whom he comes into contact. He blames his mother's overwhelming dependency on him for his behaviour.

William's mother feels intensely guilty about "trashing" William's life. As she is old and infirm she is dependent on her son and admits to a certain extent that she is reluctant to "let William go", in the way she did with his older brother who is straight and married with children.

Eventually William's mother dies and William, finding himself alone in the world with a trail of disgruntled ex-partners and disastrous relationships behind him, takes his own life.

William himself, without realizing it, created the mutual dependency situation with his mother. He, in fact, was entirely emotionally dependent on her, and could not face the world without her "maternal comfort blanket", a situation which she appeared to exploit in the face of a poor marriage and few friends. However, she was also responding to William's inability to function as a mature adult.

~   ~   ~

Freud believed that the basis of homosexuality was an "unresolved Oedipus Complex" where the fear of castration remained with the boy all of his life. He made the observation that homosexual men had (s)mothering mothers or hostile or distant fathers.

It has been speculated that there is a possibility of homosexuality being inherited, based on research and genetics. It may be the case that fathers detect homosexuality in their sons at an early age which makes them hostile and/or distant. In turn the mothers may compensate their sons for their lack of loving fathering by being "over-doting".

Blaming communication patterns

Most often this takes the form of a parent blaming a child for what is wrong in their life. Usually this takes the form of martyrdom.

- ❖ **Mother to daughter**: *"I could have had a professional career if I hadn't had to look after you"*

- ❖ **Mother to daughter**: *"you were conceived before the days of abortion on demand, I never wanted children"*

- ❖ **Father to son:** *"I never had all the nice things you've got. I've got a heart condition through working so hard to pay for them"*

- ❖ **Father to son**: *"I had to do this dreadful job for money for your up-keep. I could have been doing something different"*

~   ~   ~

Jackie has two children two years apart – a boy and a girl. She also works part-time. As her children are of slightly different ages and different sexes, they both make competing demands on her. She also has the pressure of her job, her employer not exactly being "child-friendly".

Jackie's husband has a rather narrow and one dimensional perspective of life – going to work, coming home, playing sport and watching TV. He also wants Jackie to watch him play sport, cook for him, do his laundry and entertain his family. He calls this "looking after him".

Jackie's energies are fragmented. This is particularly the case with her husband, who is very immature, being in direct competition with his children for Jackie's time, love and affection. It is often the case that he deliberately creates situations which conflict with the two competing demands of their children, whilst making little or no input into their upbringing as a father.

There have also been numerous occasions where one of the children has been sick and Jackie has found herself the victim not just of an unsympathetic boss but also an unsympathetic husband.

In this situation, Jackie feels she is in a no-win situation. She has no time for herself and her energy levels are completely sapped by the extreme competition within her family for her time and attention.

Jackie keeps trying to explain to her husband how stressful her life is particularly when she is too tired for sex and especially as he insists that is necessary for her to keep a job to help out with the family finances.

Jackie's husband is dissatisfied with the lack of a sex life so he starts an affair and makes it obvious to Jackie what he is doing. Jackie reacts to this by becoming increasingly depressed, which causes the children to start behaving very badly. Their father then spends more and more time away from home.

Jackie's continued absences from work because of her depressed mental state, the appalling state of the house and the unruly and disruptive behaviour of the children create the deciding factor for Jackie's husband who then leaves to set up home with the other woman.

Jackie plumbs the depths of depression and her parents take the children into their home. They then assist Jackie in divorcing her husband, who then finds himself in severe financial difficulties, having to pay substantial maintenance to Jackie and the children and also to keep his new woman in expensive clothes, jewellery and meals out in restaurants to maintain her affections.

Jackie's husband has created this situation, but he feels extremely sorry for himself, constantly complaining about the poor state of his finances.

The children, who are 6 years and 8 years old, blame themselves for the breakdown of their parents' marriage. Their behaviour reflects their state of mind and they are disruptive at school and performing very badly in their academic work.

~   ~   ~

Manipulating communication patterns

These are designed to control

> Mavis is devious and manipulative. She has a low IQ but what she lacks in intelligence she makes up for by manipulating people. She controls other members of her family using her favourite power mechanism – emotional blackmail.
>
> She plays members of her family off against each other so that they are in competition with each other to do the best for her. This creates disputes and tensions between other family members, but also makes Mavis the centre of attention. The members of her family are made to feel sorry for Mavis who cannot cope with any problems in her life on her own and she has to recruit her grown-up children into shouldering the burden of her problems, which are self-induced. The reality is that Mavis does not want her problems solved, but revels in martyrdom. As soon as a problem is solved she creates a new one just for the sheer attention it brings.
>
> Mavis enjoys seeing her children competing with each other to help her as she sees this as sign of their love for her, instead of the guilt which prompts their assistance.

~   ~   ~

In many marriages the husband or wife may hold the other party to ransom – only giving love and attention at the expense of a relationship with another family member i.e. mother, son, daughter, sister or brother. The husband or wife is then torn in conflict between a marriage partner and their other loved one.

This also happens in other types of family situations and is a particularly vicious way of operating.

Emma is the eldest of three daughters. Evelyn is the middle child and Jane the youngest. Emma gets news that her father has been taken to hospital with an advanced malignant brain tumour. The daughters live in the south of England whilst Albert and his wife, Edith, live in the north-west.

It is apparent that Albert has a very short time to live. Because of scarce State provision Emma and Jane feel his best interests would be served by admitting him to a private nursing home in the south, particularly in view of the fact that his wife, Edith is staying with Evelyn, and that Albert has £26,000 in savings, half of which being sufficient to pay for his care, with all the advantages and comforts that the private sector can offer. At this stage Albert is blind in one eye, going blind in the other eye and is paralysed down one side with severe memory loss and poor brain functioning.

Emma takes consolation in the fact that in this very distressing set of circumstances she and her sisters are working as a team. Emma offers psychological support to her mother, Jane liaises with medical staff and Evelyn is granted Power of Attorney over Albert's life savings. Jane then organizes for Albert to be admitted to a private nursing home and Emma makes the administrative arrangements with the nursing home. Evelyn then decides against this particular nursing home and cancels it.

Evelyn organizes a different nursing home and again arrangements are made to bring Albert down with a nurse escort, and again at the last minute, this nursing home is cancelled by Evelyn who "ducks and dives" when she is asked to explain what is going on. Her phone line is persistently on "answer phone" mode and her mobile phone has intermittent functioning. When she is requested to give an answer to a question regarding the ongoing situation, her phone contact "breaks up". Her reaction to being put on the spot is "unavailability".

Eventually a third nursing home is organized and Emma and Jane are categorically assured that Albert will be admitted there. The day before Albert is due to arrive and all transport arrangements have been formalized, Evelyn again cancels the nursing home. It is now blatantly clear that Evelyn has no intention of parting with any of her father's money to pay for his health care. When Emma is informed of this, she leaves a message on Evelyn's answer phone, which forcefully conveys her insistence that their father's admission arrangements remain intact.

To compound Edith's existing distress, Evelyn then repeatedly plays the message to her mother and then threatens Emma with the police. Albert is admitted to the nursing home where he dies four days later but the contract is never signed.

Family members try to contact Edith at Evelyn's home during this period only to be greeted by the answer phone: this remains the scenario after Albert's funeral. Contact is attempted in writing but other family members are unsure as to whether the letters have reached Edith's eyes.

After the funeral Evelyn returns Edith to her marital home in the northwest of England and Emma organizes NHS support for her. As soon as this is done, Evelyn brings Edith back to her home and a game of "musical chairs" is played with Edith and Emma who is trying to offer support.

Edith is then moved to sheltered accommodation by Evelyn. Only Emma is permitted to know her address and phone number and is "prohibited" from informing other family members. The rest of the family are upset and angry at this situation. Shortly after this Emma is then "deterred" from having contact with her mother and Jane is threatened into "staying away". Evelyn obtains a legal "Complete Authority" over Edith's life.

Evelyn warns off all family members interfering in Edith's care and welfare, abusing Emma both verbally and in writing when she requests that Evelyn seek medical attention for their mother. When Evelyn fails to do this Emma becomes involved with the health care professionals, as Edith's health is deteriorating rapidly. Edith nearly dies of malnutrition whilst being treated for depression.

Emma discovers that the scattering of Albert's ashes has been delegated to the cemetery staff as Evelyn is too busy at work to do this. However, she fails to notify either of her two sisters. On learning of this, Emma decides to scatter rose petals on her father's family rose garden at the cemetery. When Emma requests the number of the rose garden from Evelyn, she refuses to tell her which one it is and has to be pressurized into parting with the information.

A memorial service is held at church for people who have died that year of which Albert is one. Neither Emma nor Jane is "permitted" to know the date, time or venue.

Emma enters into correspondence with Evelyn on the subject of her behaviour only to be told her complaints are incoherent ramblings with Evelyn inflating her own merits. To add to Edith's existing emotional distress all communications from Emma are shown to Edith, which she finds profoundly upsetting.

Evelyn is a second child. She remembers vividly how she had to wear her older sister's cast off clothing and had to ride her sister's second-hand bike. As an adult she wants money. She is already a wealthy woman, but no amount of money is enough. Her psychological disorder compels her to accumulate more and more wealth from any source that is available.

There is no concept of morality involved in any of her actions. It is her need for love and acceptance which she feels is lacking in her life which makes her greedy and materialistic, but it is her greed for money which in fact makes her unloved and rejected. Both of her sisters have disowned her. Evelyn's only solace and security in life is the size of her bank balance.

Evelyn's behaviour is obsessive and she has very strong psychopathic traits to her personality. Evelyn has a high-pressured job with a large budget and she sees every aspect of her life, including the death of her father, as an extension of the workplace.

Evelyn feels the need to wield power over everyone. Anyone who challenges her "authority" is crushed underfoot. She is a "control freak". This is a defence against anxiety. She has been tense and anxious all of her life which is combined with a strong sense of emotional insecurity. By trying to control everyone and everything in her environment, she is trying to keep her emotional anxieties under control, and increase her sense of self-esteem.

Evelyn is arrogant and condescending – this is a defence against overwhelming feelings of inferiority. Evelyn plays games with people in order to control them and her environment. She does this by "ducking and diving" and running away. She gets pleasure from manipulating people and causing them severe distress but when she is confronted with her behaviour, feigns indignation and then makes herself unavailable for further comment. When things go wrong in her life she displays "histrionics" – becoming a "drama queen" flopping around in floods of tears and playing to a carefully selected audience.

Evelyn enjoys the power of "dangling people on a piece of string". This is a power that she didn't have as a child. Being the middle daughter of three she felt that the eldest, "the first born" had seniority and the youngest "the baby" was well protected. Evelyn had to compete on two fronts – feeling left out. She never had anything new; she had her older sister's cast-offs whilst watching her younger sister have everything new.

On the surface, Evelyn appears to be confident and assertive, but in fact she is a seething mass of insecurities caused by deep-seated feelings of anger, resentment, alienation and an overwhelming sense of emotional rejection.

Evelyn persists with her obsessive behaviour, being impervious to reason. She invalidates the feelings of people she has hurt by dismissing their complaints – in fact she is dismissive of any information which doesn't fit in with her mental "frame of reference". This is an ego-defence for her own low self-esteem.

~   ~   ~

Schizophrenia

> *"I do not know whether I was a man dreaming*
> *I was a butterfly or whether I was a butterfly*
> *Dreaming that I am a man"*

Chuang Tse
Chinese philosopher

The eminent Psychiatrist, R D Laing, claimed in his book *"The Facts of Life"* that:

❖ "there's nothing that affects our chemistry more immediately than other people"

❖ "walking into a room where we feel unwelcome creates a fluttering heart, erratic breathing, sweating palms, a dry throat and butterflies in our stomachs"

❖ "I am sure that there is a chemistry of acute fear and chronic despair".

~   ~   ~

Medical science has found chemical imbalances in the brains of schizophrenics and Dr Laing believed that these are caused by disturbing family interactions.

Schizophrenia generally starts in adolescence or early childhood, but it is possible that in some cases it may start as early as childhood or be delayed into middle age or later. Working class and black people are more likely to be diagnosed as schizophrenic than white, middle class people

Schizophrenics have difficulty processing words and images and they find it hard to distinguish between what is relevant or irrelevant.

Schizophrenia has been observed to run in families but despite searching for a gene for this illness, none has been identified to date. Personality types are believed to have a large inherited component. The "schizoid" personality type, which is likely to be inherited, is sensitive and intellectual and schizophrenia may emerge when that person is struggling to cope with bad life experiences.

There is evidence that the onset of this illness is often preceded by stressful life events and that relapses are more common in schizophrenics living with relatives who constantly pick fault with them.

Dr Laing believed that schizophrenia and the related psychosis are a natural way of "healing our appalling state of emotional alienation called normality".

⁓   ⁓   ⁓

"May you live in interesting times"

(Old Chinese curse)

Gregory Bateson believes that psychosis is a "voyage of discovery which is only completed when a person returns to the normal world." The psychotic comes back with insights that normal people would not have. He believed that:

the psychotic encounters circumstances in family life which
are so grossly maladjusted that they retreat into a
state of experiencing hallucinations.

Dr Laing stated that in all of the studies he has made of schizophrenics:

their behaviour has been shown to be a direct reaction

to an extremely abnormal and disturbed

family situation.

He claimed that in over 100 cases he and his co-workers studied:

without exception, the behaviour that gets labelled

"schizophrenic" is a special strategy that a person

invents in order to live in an unliveable situation.

Dr Laing set up a project called the Philadelphia Association in London from 1965 - 82 where disturbed people were taken out of abnormal social situations and where they were provided with accommodation and allowed to live the way they wanted to. These people sustained a substantial improvement in the state of their mental health.

Eric Berne believed that the schizophrenic is bewildered and has no functioning "Parent mode" and very little functioning "Adult mode" and so has to cope with the world in the state of mind of a "Confused child".

~   ~   ~

People living with a paranoid schizophrenic will be acutely aware of the fact that this person has something seriously wrong with them. Their behaviour will be bizarre and they will be obviously out of touch with reality. They will be hallucinating and experiencing delusions which can be threatening.

Symptoms of paranoid schizophrenia

> Delusions – believing things to be true when they are not
>
> Hallucinations – seeing or hearing things that are not there
>
> Disorganized speech – talking "mumbo-jumbo"
>
> Disorganized behaviour – such as continually pacing the floor
>
> Talking in an emotionally flat monotone voice

Schizophrenia, particularly paranoid schizophrenia, requires expert Psychiatric help at the earliest possible opportunity. The sooner treatment starts the more likely it will be effective.

～　　　～　　　～

Maria's father left home when she was 5 years old and her mother "held on" to her psychologically, purely and simply because Maria was all she had. During adolescence Maria tried to break free of her mother's control. Her mother wanted her as a "husband substitute" and for them to live together virtually as "man and wife", with Maria going out in the world everyday and her mother being there for her when she got home from work, cooking her dinner for her and doing her laundry. At weekends she would organize joint outings for both of them.

Eventually, apart from feeling her life was controlled, Maria believed that her thoughts were being controlled by outside forces and Communists were telling her to kill her mother. The very few boyfriends that Maria had in the run-up to her illness became seriously discouraged by Maria's mother and then were deterred completely by her illness.

～　　　～　　　～

Undifferentiated schizophrenia

A person with undifferentiated schizophrenia can show symptoms which are an extreme extension of normal behaviour.

❖ A religious person may believe God is instructing them to do certain works on earth

❖ They may feel unable to function in everyday life

❖ They may avoid social contact and start to be totally self-absorbed.

～　　　～　　　～

Ivor is the youngest of four children and was always quiet and introverted. He found it difficult to make friends, had poor self-confidence and low self-esteem. His life mainly revolved around going to school and then coming home to his mother. His mother encouraged a strong mother/son relationship as she did not gain any satisfaction from her marriage.

Ivor is extremely lonely man and his hobbies and interests are those of a solitary nature such as fishing and painting soldier figurines. Ivor is very emotional, insecure and sensitive. Even in adulthood he lacks the confidence to form relationships. The only relationship that makes him feel emotionally secure is the one he has with his mother.

Ivor has suddenly become intensely religious, where before he was a "rampant atheist" – being very "anti-Christians".

Ivor believes very strongly and sincerely that he has been chosen by God to rid the world of evil. Everyday he feels it necessary to do battle with "Satan".

Ivor's cousin has volunteered the opinion "When you talk to God it's called praying – when he talks back it's called schizophrenia".

~   ~   ~

However, there is a brain disorder called Temporal Lobe Epilepsy where the sufferer can hear voices. This part of the brain is associated with hearing. Van Gogh is believed to have suffered from Temporal Lobe Epilepsy and he cut off his ear in an attempt to stop the voices in his head.

When the temporal lobe of the brain has been electrically stimulated, normally sane and non-religious people have had "religious experiences" which stop as soon as the electrical stimulation is removed.

Temporal Lobe Epilepsy is not considered to be a mental illness.

~   ~   ~

A lot of research was carried out in the 1950s and 1960s into the relationship between schizophrenia and family relationships, based on the fact that Psychotherapists had started to notice that if their patients could be described as disturbed, then the families they came from could be described as disturbing.

❖ The original focus of blame was placed on mothers

❖ The next focus was on the mother's husband as a source of the problem

❖ The husband and wife interactions of the schizophrenic's parents were then examined

❖ Next the Psychotherapists looked at the parent/child relationship

❖ The nuclear family group of parents and children together was then studied

❖ Finally all the significant people in and around the family were examined.

~   ~   ~

An American Sociologist called Ervin Goffman claimed that people are usually observed "out of context" and that it is the context in which a person functions that affects his or her behaviour.

He believed that is difficult to draw a clear cut line between normal people and mental patients: well-adjusted people were just at one end of a line and the "full-fledged" psychotic was at the other end. The point at which a "normal person" could be described as psychotic is blurred.

~   ~   ~

Research has shown that families with low levels of positive, nurturing and caring behaviour, or at the other extreme where the child feels stifled and smothered, will create individuals with psychological problems.

Children who are brought up in families with negative and aggressive behaviour patterns will suffer damage to their mental health – they will become aggressive, delinquent or schizophrenic.

Five types of bad family functioning:

❖ negative behaviour patterns – these mainly focus on criticising bad behaviour as opposed to praising good behaviour

❖ parents do not recognize or encourage small improvements in a desired behaviour

❖ parents use inconsistent discipline

❖ there are low levels of positive contact: the parents are not warm and affectionate towards their child

❖ the parents aggressively emphasize their power over their child.

These bad parenting techniques then cause the child to have difficulties in forming good relationships even at an early age. The child becomes dependent, aggressive or withdrawn.

Distressed and unhappy families have "ritualized" behaviour patterns.

~   ~   ~

I believe that there is a very strong element of repressed homosexuality associated with schizophrenia, particularly in men. Often the parenting situation of (s)mothering, combined with a hostile or distant father, which is present with homosexuality, is also present in schizophrenic situations.

Mothers are often blamed for causing schizophrenia – there has been observed to be an "abnormally close" mother-child bond. However, I consider that the child who goes on to become schizophrenic creates the dependency situation and the mother is just responding to the needs of her, albeit grown-up, child.

Kevin's parents are continually at loggerheads but there is no direct discussion of the problem – just very strong undercurrents. His parents can go on for months on end without speaking to each other but communicate by asking their son to pass notes between them.

Often the cause of the disharmony is very trivial, mainly relating to minor domestic issues which could easily be resolved by a few minutes discussion. There is invariably a very bad atmosphere in the house and Kevin's mother recruits him as an ally against his father. His father responds by being hostile to Kevin, whose only crime is to do as his mother asks.

Kevin himself would prefer not to be involved, but because his father has never really shown him much love or warmth, mainly focusing on his business matters, he has become very attached to, and emotionally dependent on, his mother. This dependency has always been reinforced by her as her relationship with the husband has always been poor.

As a male, Kevin would very much like to identify with his father and adopt him as a rôle model, but finds his father is either indifferent or totally rejecting at Kevin's attempts to have a good relationship with him.

Kevin feels torn apart as his mother has obvious character faults and his father has some very good qualities.

Kevin has serious problems with his mental functioning. He has no friends and never goes out. He gave up work in his early 20s because of "nervous problems" – severe anxiety and depression which rendered him virtually unable to function.

He sees his rôle in life as being his mother's protector. His mother sees her rôle in life as looking after her son.
Kevin finds himself sexually attracted to men, but he is "asexual" – not having any form of personal relationship, but contents himself with solitary hobbies such as painting soldier figurines.

~   ~   ~

Roger is homosexual, a drug addict and very violent. Roger claims that he, like his father, served in the military and has killed people in the line of duty.

Roger has two distinct, but separate sets of very strong emotions about his actions: at one extreme he feels deep guilt and remorse – at the other extreme he intellectually justifies what he has done as being under orders.

He is very emotionally volatile and tends to explode into acts of severe violence at the slightest provocation. He puts this down to his experiences in the military. However, looking at Roger's handwriting he displays extremely brutal instinctive drives.

There's a big element of cause and effect here. It is possible that Roger joined the military in order to satisfy his need to commit acts of brutality and that he is in fact a psychopathic, feeling no remorse for the people he killed – just pretending to.

Another perspective to be seriously considered is that Roger's father related to him as a child, detailed accounts of his experiences in the military which shocked Roger's young mind and he had difficulty getting the memories out of his head.

It may well be that Roger has a very severe mental illness and was never in the Army. It is possible that he has somehow absorbed his father's identity and truly believes he was in the military and committed acts of violence.

It is also possible that Roger was sexually abused as a child, and has absorbed his father's strength as a military man in trying to identify with his father by "stealing" his identity, in order to feel some power.

Roger also believes himself to be adopted.

~   ~   ~

With schizophrenic people, there is a fragmentation of the personality: there is no connection between the emotional and intellectual components of the personality. Alice Miller believes that schizophrenia can arise from sexual abuse in childhood. She believes that being psychotic is a way of trying to communicate the pain of a disturbing and damaging childhood.

Schizophrenia is a very serious mental illness.

~   ~   ~

Obsessive Compulsive Disorder

This illness involves the sufferer experiencing abnormal and unrealistic thoughts and fears. These people are obsessed by certain ideas and feel compelled to act on them.

They believe that harm will come to them or their loved ones if certain rituals aren't performed.

Obsessional thoughts include

❖ fear of exposure to germs and dirt

❖ fear that something bad will happen to them if the task has not been completed "correctly"

❖ hypochondria: the unrealistic fear of having a serious life-threatening disease

❖ the need to have certain objects in a certain position

❖ recurrent obsessive thoughts that they have committed a violent crime

❖ repeatedly distressing thoughts about impulses to perform inappropriate sexual behaviours, associated with overwhelming feelings of shame and guilt.

In its extreme form obsessive-compulsive disorder may become obsessional neurosis and prevent the suffer from leading a normal life.

Obsessive compulsive disorder can be treated by Psychologists with Behaviour Modification techniques.

Eating Disorders

Psychologists believe that there may be a connection between bulimia and "body shame" caused by childhood abuse – which can be either physical or emotional, or both.

Food has been connected with love. It is possible that good basic food such a hotpot or roast dinner could resemble mother love. Many people talk of "comfort eating", which can be a substitute for love. Food can be a mother's way of showing love of her child.

Bulimia is an eating disorder involving binge-eating and then vomiting. Bulimics are thought to lack the control over their eating that anorexics have.

The bulimic may simultaneously experience the need for food in the form of mother love, and then reject it because of bad mother/child experiences.

Fiona has been bulimic since being teased at school about her weight. Her relationship with her mother is also at its lowest point, mainly due to the fact that Fiona finds her "over controlling" behaviour to be psychologically repressive and suffocating. Her mother loves her very much but allows her no independence of action or opinion.

Fiona realizes she can get thin by vomiting after every meal. She feels emotionally on an "even keel" if her stomach is completely empty. She may well feel she is happy being emotionally and psychologically empty – free from her mother's control.

~   ~   ~

Luxury foods such as chocolate have been noticed to produce similar brain chemistry to when we are in love. Images of attractive women provocatively eating certain brands of food is an obvious example of the link between sex and food.

Anorexia has been linked with obsessive-compulsive disorder and I believe that there is a link between traumatic childhood experiences and this very serious eating disorder. There is a strong possibility that they are obsessed by food and compelled to refuse it.

In its milder form the person with obsessive-compulsive disorder will constantly check and recheck to see if they have locked doors when they go out.

In Freudian terms this behaviour has strong sexual connections: a door is the way into a house and is symbolized by the subconscious as the vagina, the house symbolising the body.

Research has shown that people suffering from obsessive-compulsive disorders have problems with some aspects of their memory and that is why they have to repeatedly check their actions. It may be that this memory loss is the mind's way of blotting out the subconscious memory of the abuse. It is believed that the use of "neutralising" thoughts or actions provides the sufferer with the ability to avoid negative thoughts regarding personal responsibility for harm.

This could be described as "cognitive avoidance" – and often the sufferer may not realize what they are doing – let alone control it.

≈   ≈   ≈

Anorexics tend to be perfectionist young women – some 90 to 95% of sufferers are female. They are intelligent and they tend to have dieting mothers. They are prone to suffer from phobias, panic attacks and major depressive symptoms.

≈   ≈   ≈

Betty has always had a rather nervous and obsessional personality. As a child she had to have her toys in a certain place, and became anxious if they were moved or changed in any way. She was also rather regimented in her behaviour, particularly in regard to her eating habits, feeling the need to eat the same foods at the same time of day on the same plate with the same knife and fork. She is intelligent and enjoys her schoolwork.

At around 10 years of age her father starts to go into her bedroom at night and manipulates her genitals. She feels a combination of guilt, fear, shame, anguish and sexual arousal, all intermingled in a blur which she believes may be a bad dream. Her emotions are scrambled by the fact that her father acts in a perfectly normal way the next day, as though nothing has happened.

This behaviour is repeated several nights a week when her mother is out playing bingo and she learns to dread going to bed. Her father appears not to be doing the same to her sister who sleeps in the next room. The father seems to have a different set of feelings, rules and standards for Hannah who he seems to have respect for.

Betty is repeatedly abused into her teens and only stops when she gets a rather "heavy" boyfriend in the age of 15. Betty has never told anybody about this as she feels she has in some way brought the abuse on herself. The reality is that Betty strongly resembles her mother, who, although she still has sexual relations with her husband, has a lot of inner hostility because of the way her husband has treated her over very many years, that is, womanising and keeping her short of money.

At around 17 Betty develops anorexia in that she perceives herself to be more powerful the thinner she becomes. She thinks that people who do not have very strict control over their food intake are weak and powerless. In Betty's opinion thin is powerful. Betty is proud of the fact that her bones show through her clothes.

Unconsciously the thinner Betty becomes more quickly she is fading away, regressing physically back through puberty and becoming a child again. In this way she is denying her sexuality, as her first ex-perience of sexual arousal was with her father, with all the emotional confusion that was associated with it.

Her obsessional rejection of food may well symbolize the rejection of love, with its associations with nourishment and protection. This is the ultimate power mechanism – rejecting "nourishment" both physi-cal and emotional.

Betty is obsessively clean; her personal hygiene and housework rou-tines have a high priority on her agenda. Betty's house is spotless and she indulges in "cleaning binges", whereby whole weekends are set aside for cleaning. She cleans the sinks in public lavatories and inspects other people's houses for signs of dirt and dust.

The obsessive cleanliness is likely to be an expression of her deep-rooted feelings of "dirtiness" caused by the sexual abuse. She feels internally "soiled" by her experience, and is trying to cleanse herself by cleaning herself and the world around her.

~   ~   ~

Obsessional cleanliness is believed to be a repressed desire to look at and ex-plore other people's genitals and is probably an unconscious way of suppressing the compulsion to repeat the behaviour experienced in childhood or adolescence.

There is a large overlap between anorexic and bulimia. One half of patients with anorexia have bulimic symptoms. One third of bulimics have a history of anorexia.

Eating disorders require expert psychiatric help.

～   ～   ～

STRESS MANAGEMENT

"It matters not how straight the gate

How charged with punishments the scroll

I am the master of my fate

I am the captain of my soul"

William Ernest Henley

If people are behaving badly towards you approach them firmly but politely with a list of your complaints.

If you feel unable to speak to them, then write them a letter expressing your dissatisfaction with their behaviour and ask them for an apology or explanation.

If you feel unable to do either of these things then write all your complaints down and then read them to yourself.

By expressing yourself on paper you are discharging negative emotions.

~   ~   ~

Think back to recent stressful events and make a note of the event that sparked off the stress.

How did you deal with the stressful situation? How would you have preferred to deal with it?

Make a list of stressful circumstances in your life and look for ways of removing them or making them less stressful.

The power of positive thinking

I intend to be happy despite you:

- ❖ I will find a hobby or interest

- ❖ I will get a new or better job

- ❖ I will refuse to let you upset me.

- ❖ I intend to acknowledge that you are the person with the problem and not me

❖ I intend to believe that I am a good person and deserve better treatment

❖ I intend to pity you for being so damaged

❖ I am like a rubber ball – the harder you push me down the higher I will bounce back.

Caroline Brazier, the Buddhist Psychotherapist, believes it is necessary to:

❖ break habit behaviours in everyday life and relationships

❖ remove cravings for people and objects

❖ let go of self-absorption

❖ love life and find something positive and enjoyable to do everyday.

Carl Rogers, a prominent Psychologist, believed we should remove:

❖ greed, hate and delusion

and replace it with

❖ straightforwardness.

Emotional intelligence

This is the ability to perceive emotions, to access and generate emotions which can assist thought. This is also the ability to have a streetwise attitude to personal and social relationships which are strong on intuition.

Self regard

This is the ability to respect and accept yourself as basically good, whilst having the ability to acknowledge your weak points. It is about having an honest and objective picture of what you are really like. This is different from self-esteem which focuses purely on pumping up the ego, which can then verge on arrogance without the necessary positive qualities to back it up.

❖ How much do like yourself?

❖ How do you rate for loyalty, humour, friendless, honesty?

❖ How do you rate for bad temper, inefficiency?

Learning empathy

Empathy is the ability to be sensitive to the way another person feels and to emotionally read them. This is different from sympathy where another person can only listen and offer comfort. In the case of living with someone with destructive character traits, empathy is valuable because you receive accurate information about that person's thoughts and feelings and it gives you a good base to work with.

Your partner may feel inferior to you and all that is required is your assistance in confidence boosting and offering them appreciation.

In the case of a Psychopath or the Emotional Vampire the information you may receive may be so unpleasant that you would wish to end the relationship.

Optimism

The Psychologist, Martin Seligman, has described three major attitudes that distinguish optimists from pessimists:

❖ they regard downturns in their lives as temporary

❖ they regard misfortunes as unfortunate one-off situations and not the road to doom

❖ they try not to shoulder all the blame for problems, looking for outside influences and causes.

Relationships

Positive interpersonal relationships are based on sensitivity towards other people. The Psychologists, Turner and Beidel, designed a programme to help people overcome social anxiety:

❖ How do you begin and end an interaction?

❖ Are you a good listener?

❖ Are you comfortable talking to a group of people? If so you stand a
better chance of having a meaningful long-term relationship.

❖ What does your friend or a family member like about you?

❖ What do they do they dislike?

Many books on personal relationships assume that we have partners who are
sane and rational, and good, decent people. This is not necessarily the case
and a person can suffer very badly by presuming their partner will respond to
communications based on a true sense of normality.

John Gray states that *"a woman's ability to give and receive love in her relationship is generally a reflection of how she is feeling about herself"*.

My contention is that a woman's ability to give and receive love in her relationship is generally a reflection of how she is feeling about the way she is being
treated by her partner.

He also refers to communicating without blame.

Why not blame?

If someone has done something wrong then blame them. Ask them for an apology and explanation.

People often assume they can brush big mistakes under the carpet – but what they should accept is that they need to earn forgiveness over a period of time.

If your partner is unresponsive in bed, don't just assume there is something wrong with you or them – look for some unresolved issue.

Don't just assume the problems are purely male/female issues. There are different levels of men and women – sometimes one of the partners needs to level up, or the other needs to level down.

Women are able to function on "pragmatism", which is a psychological list of good or bad qualities in a partner which is completely devoid of emotion and purely an intellectual quality. Unfortunately there is very little emotional satisfaction in relationships like this and I believe the psyche may be disturbed.

This may create psychosomatic illness such as neuroses and stress-related disorders such as irritable bowel syndrome, sleeping problems and mood changes.

Repressing anger is also profoundly damaging psychologically and physically and this can create illness.

The build up of anger needs to be released and if it is bottled up can lead to illnesses such as high blood pressure, asthma and migraine.

~   ~   ~

SELF-HEALING

"O, happy wind, how sweet
Thy life must be!
The great, proud fields of gold
Run after thee:
And here are flowers, with heads
To nod and shake;
And dreaming butterflies
To tease and wake.
Oh, happy wind, I say,
To be alive this day"

William Henry Davis

According to the 19th century Philosopher, William James, our state of mind is never precisley the same. Experience is remoulding us every moment and our reaction to everything is based on our experiences up to that date.

Childhood Guilt

Children under the age of eight years tend to blame themselves for all the ills of the family – this is believed to be carried through into their adult life. If you are in a destructive relationship and had an unhappy childhood, probably with warring parents, then it is likely you will blame yourself for the problems in the relationship.

A Psychologist called Wilhelm Reich believed that:

> ❖ **people build up systems of "body armouring" in response to painful childhood experiences.**

> ❖ **this can take the form of not allowing people to get too close to you physically and emotionally.**

Caroline Brazier has put a Buddhist perspective on psychotherapy and is in the process of developing "Buddhist Psychology".

She believes it is necessary to:

> ❖ **recognize guilt for childhood misdemeanours**

> ❖ **recognize this guilt in a "clean way".**

She maintains that:

> ❖ **anger is produced by fear, hate and grief**

> ❖ **repressed anger can create depressive states.**

And that it is important to

> ❖ **recognize the painful emotions responsible for our anger**

> ❖ **express anger in an acceptable way to relieve tension.**

Anxiety
Understanding the symptoms of anxiety

> ❖ the feelings are nothing more than exaggeration of the normal bodily reactions to stress

> ❖ they are unpleasant but not harmful

> ❖ by having frightening thoughts about what is happening, you are making the situation worse.

Coping with anxiety

> ❖ accept what is happening to you – don't fight it or run away – the fear will pass

> ❖ take the middle finger of one hand and place it in the centre of the palm of the other hand. Move it in firm circular movements to the outside of the palm and then back into the centre again. Repeat this until you are feeling calmer.

> ❖ press firmly with the thumb on the area between the thumb and first finger on the other hand. Release and repeat. (This is an acupressure point).

> ❖ breathe into a **paper** bag. This increases the carbon dioxide in the blood. (Anxiety creates too much oxygen in the blood).

> ❖ imagine yourself breathing in calmness and breathing out tension.

DO NOT DO THIS IF YOU SUFFER OR HAVE SUFFERED FROM EPILEPSY

Put on some relaxing music and focus your attention on a spot directly in the centre of your eyebrows.

Imagine yourself in a very relaxing environment of your choice. This could be a favourite garden.

Try to get your mental state into one of drowsy relaxation.

Make a list of positive suggestions for your well-being.

DO NOT USE NEGATIVE SUGGESTIONS - ONLY POSITIVE SUGGESTIONS

These can be:
- ❖ **I will be more confident**

- ❖ **I will be more assertive**

- ❖ **I will be more relaxed**

- ❖ **I will be able to cope with stress**

Right living

**Eastern philosophy has described the concept of
"dis-ease". This is a disturbance of emotions and
the disharmony of mind which creates illness.**

Buddhists refer to the bad effects of having our behaviour conditioned (samsara) and believe that it is possible to break free of this by initiating positive change.

Buddhism is the philosophy that most embodies the concept of healing. It embraces the concept of "wholeness".

Buddhism aims to rule out the general feelings of dissatisfaction that many people feel are pervading their lives. These negative feelings can cause acute distress and illness.

The name given to the dissatisfaction and negative thought process is called "Dukkha" and this is often expressed by selfish desire which has strong connections with ignorance, greed and hatred.

In turn, the lack of ability to satisfy the selfish desires felt, makes a person's life unsatisfactory, and so a vicious circle is created.

To break this vicious circle, and to heal the damage created by destructive people and relationships, it could be useful to adopt what is known in Buddhist circles as:

The Noble Eightfold Path

Right understanding – acknowledging that life has

    ❖ Impermanence

    ❖ unsatisfactoriness

Right thought – acknowledging the power of the mind

    ❖ positive thoughts

    ❖ loving kindness

    ❖ compassion.

Right speech – being truthful and abstaining from gossip.

Right action – doing good.

    ❖ not taking life

    ❖ not stealing

    ❖ not engaging in sexual misconduct.

Right livelihood – have a good quality job which

    ❖ does not involve hurting others

    ❖ does not involve destroying life.

Right effort – think carefully about

    ❖ what we do

    ❖ what we say.

Right awareness – taking care to be in life

> ❖ entirely awake

> ❖ entirely alert.

Right concentration – this is necessary for

> ❖ a deeper level of attentiveness

> ❖ peace and calm.

This can be achieved by meditation, which develops "mindfulness" starting with greater consciousness of ourselves, our minds, our bodies and emotions. This positive psychological state will radiate out to other people and the surrounding environment.

Close your eyes and centre your attention on your body contact with the chair or floor. Breathe slowly and gently. Repeat to yourself:

> ❖ May I be free from fear
> ❖ May I be happy
> ❖ May I be at peace.

〜   〜   〜

> *"Love suffers long and is kind*
> *love does not envy; love does not parade*
> *itself; it is not puffed up; does not seek its own;*
> *is not provoked, thinks no evil, does not rejoice in injustice, but*
> *rejoices in the truth; bears all things...*
> *and endures all things"*

> *Corinthians*

In order to truly heal ourselves from the destructive nature of damaging relation-ships, it is necessary:

- ❖ to understand the nature of the problem

- ❖ to distance ourselves physically and psychologically from their influ-ence and behaviour

- ❖ to avoid retaliation and revenge

- ❖ to gain strength through weakness

- ❖ to learn to love ourselves and have a positive attitude towards our-selves

- ❖ to realize good self-regard is influential in forming good relationships with other people.

**FUNDAMENTAL TO HEALING THE EXPERIENCES OF
BAD PERSONAL RELATIONSHIPS IT IS NECESSARY
TO RECOGNIZE THE SYMPTOMS OF THE
PSYCHOLOGICALLY DISTURBED
INDIVIDUAL WHO IS DAMAGING
AND DESTRUCTIVE**

~　　　~　　　~

**FUNDAMENTAL TO HEALING BAD FAMILY
EXPERIENCES IS TO RECOGNIZE THAT IT IS
A SIGN OF MATURITY TO FORGIVE OUR PARENTS,
SEEING THEM AS FALLIBLE HUMAN BEINGS.**

In order to be better people ourselves it is necessary to realize that although we are moulded by our heredity and childhood experiences we can choose to be the people we want to be

WE HAVE THE CAPACITY FOR FREE WILL

When you reach the heart of life
you shall find beauty in
all things

Kahlil Gibran

≈   ≈   ≈

REFERENCES

Adler AC – *"The neurotics picture of the World"* – International Journal of Psychology – Harcourt Brace Jarovich – New York (1936).

Alexander F – *"Psychosomatic Medicine"* – Norton – New York (1950).

Andrews, Bernice – *"Family"* – University of London (1997).

APA (1994).

Argyle MC – *"The Social Psychology of Work"* (2nd edn) (1989).

Ballard CG, Mohan RN, Handy S – *"Chronic depersonalization neurosis au Shorvon: a successful intervention"* – British Journal of Psychiatry 160 123-125 (1992).

Baron M, Risch N, Levitt M & Gruen R – *"Familial transmission of schizotypal and borderline personality disorders"* – American Journal of Psychiatry 142 927-934 (1985)

Bartels A and Zeki S – *"The neural basis of romantic love"* – Neuroreport 17 3829-3834 (2000).

Berne – *"Games People Play"* – Penguin – London (1964).

Bernstein EM and Putnam FW – *"Development reliability and validity of a dissociation scale"* – Journal of Nervous and Mental Disease 174 727-735 (1986).

Blueler E – *""Dementia Praecox" of the Group of Schizophrenics"* – (trans J.Zinkin) – New York (1950).

Bowlby JC – *"Maternal Care and Mental Health"* – World Health Organization [includes comment on the nature of the relationship which child needs with mother] – Geneva – (1952).

Bowlby JC – *"Attachment and Loss – Vol1"* – Penguin Harmondsworth (1971).

Brazier, Caroline – *"Buddhist Psychology"* – Constable and Robinson – London (2003).

Bus DM & Shakelford TK – *"Relation of sex and gender to love, sexual attitudes and self-esteem"* – Journal of Research in Personality 31 193-221 (1997).

Chu JA and Dill DL – *"Dissociative symptoms in relation to childhood physical and sexual abuse"* – American Journal of Psychiatry 147 887-892 (1990).

Checkley HE – *"The Mask of Sanity"* – St Louis Mosby (1976).

Cloninger CR et al – *"Personality Disorders"* – in Guze SB – *"Adult Psychiatry"* – New York – Mosby (1997).

Craft MJ – *"Ten Studies into Psychopathic Personality"* – Bristol (1965).

Curran D and Mallinson P – *"Psychopathic Personality"* – Journal of Mental Science 90 266ff (1944).

Derksen J – *"Personality Disorders, Clinical and Social Perspectives"* – John Wiley – Chichester (1995).

De Vries K & Miller D – *"Unstable at the Top"* – Signet – New York (1987).

Dworkin. Andrea.

Eysenck HJ – *"Graphological Analysis and Psychiatry: an Experimental Study"* – British Journal of Psychology 35 70-81.

Field T – *"Interaction behaviours of primary versus secondary caretakers (fathers)"* – Developmental Psychology 14 183-185 (Father's rôle in childcare) (1978).

Freud S – *"Introductory Lectures in Psychoanalysis Vol1"* – Pelican Freud Library – Penguin Harmondsworth (1973).

Gray J – *"Men are from Mars, Women are from Venus"* – Element Thorsons (Harper Collins) – London (1992).

Greer, Germaine – *"The Female Eunuch"* – Granada Publishing Ltd (1970).

Gunderson JG & Saban AN – *"The phenomenological and conceptual interface between borderline personality disorder and PTSD"* – American Journal of Psychiatry 150 19-27 (1993).

Hamer Dean – *"Science"* – US National Cancer Institute (1993).

Hare RD, Harper TJ, Hakstian RA, et al – *"The revised Psychopathy Checklist: Reliability and Factor Structure: Psychological Assessment* (1990).

Harlow HF and Harlow MK – *"Social Deprivation in Monkeys"* – Scientific American, November, Reprint No 473 [The inability of female monkeys in isolation to care for offspring] (1962).

Hendrick S and Hendrick C – *"Multidimensionality of Sexual Attitudes"* – The Journal of Sex Research 502-506 (1987).

Hendrick C, Hendrick S, Foote F and Slapian-Foote M – *"Do men and women love differently?"* – Journal of Social and Personal Relationships (1) 177-196 (1984).

Henderson D – *"Psychopathic States"* – New York (1939).

Herbert M – *"Discipline: A positive guide for parents"* – [The positive why's and wherefores of discipline] – Basil Blackwell – Oxford (1989).

Hoek HW – *"The distribution of eating disorder"* – in KD Brownell & CG Fairburn (Eds) – *"Eating disorders and obesity"* – A Comprehensive handbook (pp207-211) – Guilford – New York (1995).

Jung CG – *"Memories, Dreams and Reflections"* – Collins RKP – London (1963).

Kagan J – *"Galen's Prophecy: Temperament in Human Nature"* – Basic Books – New York (1994).

Kennedy SH and Garfinkel PE – *"Advances in the diagnosis and treatment of anorexia and bulimia nervosa"* – Canadian Journal of Psychiatry 37, 309-315 (1992).

Kernberg OF – *"Borderline Personality organisation"* – Journal of the American Psychoanalysis Association 15641-85 (1967).

Kernberg OF – *"Borderline conditions and pathological narcissism"* – Northvale NJ – Jason Aronson *(1985).*

Kety SS, Rosenthal D, Wender PH & Schulsinger F – *"Mental Illness in the biological and adoptive families of adopted schizophrenics"* – American Journal of Psychiatry 128 82-86 (1971).

Kohlberg L – *"Moral Stages and Moralization"* – in T Likana (Ed) Moral Development and Behaviour – Holt – New York (1976).

Laing RD – *"The Politics of Experience"* and *"The Bird of Paradise"* – Penguin Harmondsworth (1967).

Linz D – *"Exposure to sexually explicit materials and attitudes towards rape"* – Journal of Sex Research 26, 50-84 (1989).

Marne, Patricia – *"Sexual Secrets in Handwriting"* – Foulsham (1988).

Mazur R – *"Beyond Jealousy and possessiveness"* – in G Clanton and L Smith (Eds) "Jealousy" – Prentice Hall, Eaglewood Cliffs, NJ (1977).

Mental Health Act (1959).

Miller A – *"The Drama of being a child"* – Virago – London (1987).

Miller A – *"For Your own Good"* – Virago – London (1987).

Miller A – *"Banished Knowledge: Facing Childhood Injuries"* – Virago – London (1990).

Nigg JT, Lohr NE, Weston D, Gold LJ & Silk KR – *"Malevolent object representations in borderline personality and major depression"* –Journal of Abnormal Psychology 101 61-67 (1992).

Nigg JT, Goldsmith JT & Goldsmith HH – *Genetics of Personality Disorders: perspectives from personality and psychopathology research"* – Psychological Bulletin 115 346-380 (1994).

Paris JC – *"Completed suicide in borderline personality disorder"* – Psychiatric Annals 20 19-21 (1990).

Rapee RM – *"Generalized anxiety disorder: A review of clinical features and theoretical concepts"* – Clinical Psychology 11, 419-440 (1991).

Robins LN – *"Deviant Children Grown Up"* – Baltimore (1966).

Rogers CP – *"Client-centred therapy: its current practices, implications and theory"* – Houghton-Mills – Boston (1951).

Rubin Z – *"Measurement of Romantic Love"* – Journal of Personality and Social Psychology – Harvard University.

Rutter M – *"Maternal Deprivation Reassessed"* – Penguin Harmondsworth.

Salkovski PM – *"Obsessional-compulsive problems: A cognitive behavioural analysis"* – Behavioural Research and Therapy 23 571-583 (1985).

Sartoli Omella – *"How to read handwriting"* – Hamlyn (1989).

Sereny Gitta – *"The case of Mary Bell"* – New York (1972).

Scheflen – *"The significance of posture in Communication systems"* – Psychiatry 27316-31 (1964).

Schneider K (trans Hamilton MW) – *"Psychopathic Personalities"* – London (1958).

Silk KR, Lee S, Hill EM & Lohr N – *"Borderline Personality Disorder Symptoms and severity of sexual abuse"* – American Journal of Psychiatry 152 1053-1057 (1995).

Singer Eric – *"A Manual of Graphology"* – Treasure Press (1986).

Spitzer RL, Endicott J & Gibbons M – *Crossing the border into borderlines personality and borderline schizophrenia"* – (1979)

Stein, Steven J – *"The EQ Edge"* – Stoddart – Canada (2001).

Stevens R – *"Freud and Psychoanalysis"* – The Open University Press – Milton Keynes.

Torgersen S – *Genetic and sociological aspects of schizotypical and borderline personality disorders"* – Archives of General Psychiatry 41 546-554 (1984).

Wakeling AC – *"Epidemiology of anorexia nervosa"* – Psychiatry Review 62 3-9 (1966).

Walker N – *"Liberty, Liability and Culpability"* – Medicine, Science and the Law – (January 1965).

Walters E and Kendler KS – *"Anorexia Nervosa and anorexia like symptoms in population based twin samples"* – American Journal of Psychiatry 152 62-71 (1994).

Whitlock FA – *"Prichard and the concept of moral insanity"* – Australian and New Zealand Journal of Psychiatry 2, 71-79. (1967).

Wiederman MW & Hurd C – *Extradyadic involvement during dating"* – Journal of Social and Personal Relationships 16 265-274 (1999).

Wing J (Ed) – *"Schizophrenia from within"* – London (1975).
Wooton B – *"Social Science and Social Pathology"* – London (1959).

Zanarini MC et al – *"Childhood experiences of borderline patients"* – Comprehensive Psychiatry 30 18-25 (1989).

Zanarini MC – *"Childhood experiences associated with the development of Borderline Personality Disorder"* – Psychiatric Clinics of North America 23 89-101 (2000).

Zanarini MC et al – *"Biparental failure in the childhood experiences of borderline patients"* – Journal of Personality Disorder 14 264-273 (2000).